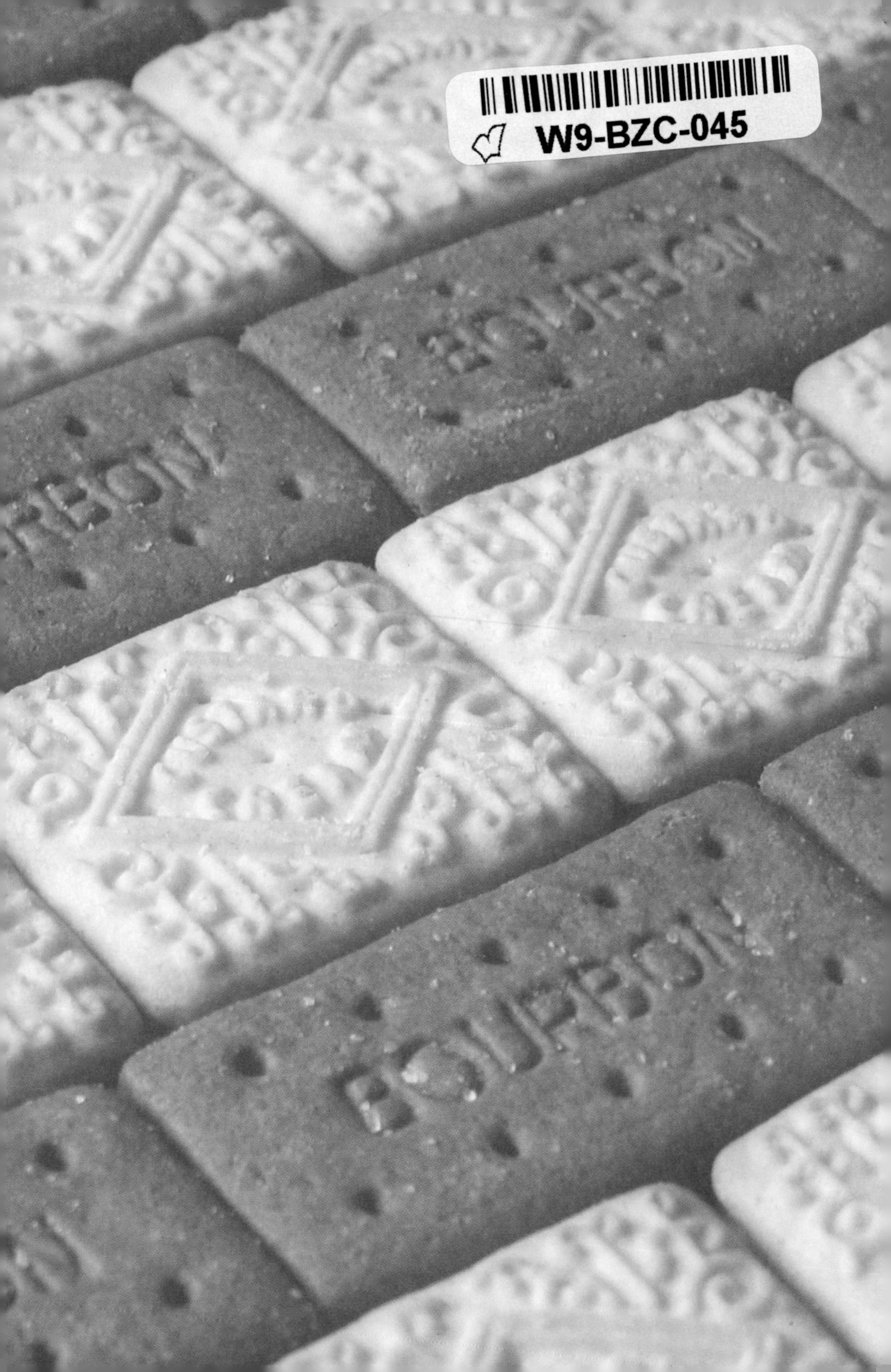
BOURBON

NICEY AND WIFEY'S

nice cup of tea and a sit down

Nicey

+

Wifey

A *Time Warner* Book

First published in Great Britain in 2004 by Time Warner Books

Reprinted 2004 (three times)

A CIP catalogue record for this book is available from the British Library.

ISBN 0 316 72917 5

Typeset in Frutiger by M Rules
Printed and bound in Great Britain by
The Bath Press, Bath

Abbey, Chukka, Crawford's, Hobnob(s), Macfarlane Lang, McVitie & Price,
McVitie's, McVitie's The Original Digestive (biscuit device), One Nibble And
You're Nobbled, P . . P . . P . . . Pick Up A . . . Penguin, Penguin, Rover, Royal
Scot, Splatz, Yoyo are all registered trade marks of United Biscuits (UK) Limited
and used with kind permission

Time Warner Books
An imprint of
Time Warner Book Group UK
Brettenham House
Lancaster Place
London WC2E 7EN

www.twbg.co.uk

For Dad
who liked a decent biscuit

Contents

A Little Bit of Cake

And a Sit Down

Introduction

Put a cup of tea in your hand and what else can you do but sit down?

There can be few more relaxing things in life than a nice cup of tea and a sit down. A good hot bath is one, but that's not always an option, especially if you are at work or doing your shopping.

Or maybe like us your bath is fairly short and small, and you have to sit bolt upright in it. If you do lie down in it then your legs have to stick out at the tap end, halfway up the wall, and they get cold. Playing loud music and drinking a glass of brandy or whiskey go some way to diverting us from the fact that our bath was designed for a lost race of people with an average height of 4ft 6ins, but it's far from ideal.

Anyway, a nice cuppa while sitting down is the cornerstone of British society, possibly even more important to us than television or queuing up for things. The cultural accoutrements of tea and sitting down are everywhere in our daily life, from cups, pots, cosies and bags to whole ladies equipped with urns given over to the service of tea. Not to mention sofas, armchairs, kitchen stools, corners of desks and sitting up against a nice plumped-up pillow in bed.

When moving house the first item to be unpacked is the electric kettle. Tea in conjunction with sitting down is so important in British culture that its consumption after unifying and world-shaping events (such as moon landings, cup finals and the shooting of J. R. Ewing) results in millions of extra kilowatts of electricity being generated to cope with ten million British households putting the kettle on. Indeed, during half-time in the recent 2003 Rugby World Cup Final there was a power spike equivalent to 850,000 kettles being simultaneously switched on.

The vast majority of sitting-down-with-a-cup-of-tea engagements would, however, be incomplete without biscuits. Indeed, tea without biscuits is a

missed opportunity. Like all great double acts, the whole is greater than the sum of its parts. On its own, the cup of tea will of course bring warmth and comforting refreshment to you but add, say, three or four Digestives and one is reinvigorated, ready to face the world anew. We can now perhaps achieve such great things as a little light housework, reading the paper, or potting on some geraniums.

Finding the perfect biscuit for the occasion is as much an art as it is a science, and has occupied most, if not all, of my tea-drinking life. In a similar way, the French have made a national pastime of choosing the right wine to go with the right dish. However, if you've ever read the labels on the wine bottles you'll see that they all seem to go with cheese, but that's probably because the French make an awful lot of that as well. There is obviously some kind of duopoly set up between the cheese makers and the vineyards. Perhaps science will eventually come up with a cheese that doesn't go with wine and a wine that doesn't go with cheese. This could then be combined to form a sauce that doesn't go well with itself, let alone anything else.

Like most of the British populace, biscuits have played a part in my life from my earliest memories. During the 1930s and 1940s, my grandparents had a small shop in the East End of London, which like all others at the time sold biscuits loose from large drums. As a young boy, my dad would help himself to the broken biscuits and developed his own keen biscuit skills, which he eventually passed on to me. Through my school years he would often discuss the merits of one biscuit over another during our daily four o'clock cuppa. So biscuit appraisal is in my blood.

I haven't set out to cover every classic biscuit in this book, or even every important biscuit that there is. Nevertheless, I seem to have covered quite a lot of them and I'm sure you'll find some of your favourites here. We all have our personal preferences for highly individual reasons and it's not just the way that they taste. Often it's to do with a time or place that they accompany us to while we munch away. To mark them out of ten would be undignified and meaningless, so I'll just share my personal thoughts on them. You might not always agree with me but then that is to be expected. I hope you will think that many have a curious personality that is worth a second look.

Tea drinkers don't tend to have moderate and liberal views on tea. We all like it the way we like it, whatever way that may be. I'm certainly not about to come up with something as doomed to failure as a pronouncement on how to make the ideal cup. If you've ever made tea for somebody else, chances are that they politely complained about it being too weak, too strong, too milky or in the wrong sort of cup. When it comes to tea, one size does not fit all. So it's not the recipe for the perfect cup of tea that I'll be discussing here but some of the obstacles that are placed in our personal path towards it.

Although it is biscuits that most often accompany our cuppas, from time to time cake pops up. So I've left space for a little bit of cake near the end as a special treat. Cake would like a much bigger bit, as it can be quite full of itself, but I've kept it down to a few slices of my favourites.

Finally, I'll take a look at some of the many and varied ways in which we pursue that relaxing sit down so crucial to a successful cup of tea. From not sitting down at a stand-up buffet to sitting on your coat while sipping tea from your vacuum flask, when tea is at hand the sit down is sought after; if we are already sitting down, then the need for tea increases. I'll look at some of the situations in which we risk scalded fingers, wet clothes, puncture wounds and instant tea, just to capitalise on our sedentary circumstances.

So here it is: forty years of biscuit eating, tea drinking and the occasional slice of cake condensed into a handy book. Much like on our website, Wifey is going to have her say, so watch yourselves. If you know the website then you'll find plenty that is new here, not least finally getting round to my thoughts on the Pink Wafer. If you don't know the site, then I hope you'll enjoy what is a personal and affectionate look at some of the simple pleasures that feature in most of our daily lives.

A Nice Cup of Tea

of Tea

 # Tea

My Worst Cup of Tea Ever

San Jose, California, May 1999. My worst cup of tea, ever, really.

This was my first visit to the USA, and my first experience of jet lag. It was also my first time filling in one of those bizarre green cards, required by American Immigration, on which you are required to declare whether or not you have ever been a member of the Nazi Party or have committed acts of genocide. Now obviously these are very important and serious questions, but how often do they actually catch people out this way? If I were a genocidal sort of character, then not ticking a box asking me to own up to it would probably be something I was capable of too. Nevertheless, I couldn't help but glance at the green cards of other passengers near to me.

On the way to America we passed over Greenland, Baffin Island (named after an old Geography teacher of mine, or it may have been the other way round) and northern Canada. None of these places seemed like anywhere where we should have tried to make a quick stop for a cuppa and a little stretch of the legs.

After eleven hours' flying we touched down in San Francisco, three hours after taking off, or something like that. It quickly became apparent that, having dealt with the Nazis, fruit and snails were the next most pressing issues for the authorities. I immediately started to feel guilty and shifty, having freely associated with both. Indeed, a couple of days earlier while digging over the vegetable patch, I had filled the bottom of a bucket with snails that had been overwintering in the garden. Had any of these hidden themselves in the seams of my clothing? When asked by the official why I was visiting the United States, it was as much as I could do to remember, given that it was way past midnight at teatime. 'For business,' I replied. 'What sort of business?' he asked. Being a *Dallas* fan, I wanted to reply, 'Da oil business', but thought it best to say I was off to a computer development convention. This did the trick and they let me in. It was a good job I didn't mention the fifty bags of PG Tips stashed in my luggage.

We stayed up until what must have been technically half past five in the morning. After a wholesome tea of melted cheese chilli sticks, washed down with carbonated brown stuff and several other things that might have been chips we retired to our beds. I awoke the next day bright and early about 6.30 a.m. local time.

After showering, there really was only one thing on my mind. Tea. Whether it was ignorance, blind optimism or a misplaced faith in the kindness of my fellow man, I left my tea bags in my hotel room and headed down for breakfast. I met my colleagues in the dining room, all seasoned visitors to the US. They were seated around a table with starched white tablecloths, napkins, silver cutlery and a large bowl of freshly prepared Californian fruit. When the waiter appeared, everyone else ordered coffee. I asked for tea; 'a nice one please'. I should have picked up on his slightly confused expression.

Pots of coffee soon arrived. In my case, however, the waiter approached carrying a large wooden box, very much like the sort one keeps one's duelling pistols in. He opened the lid to show me the contents but rather than guns, it contained an array of unlikely and very dud-looking tea bags. Trying to take control over my general state of disorientation I carefully scanned the contents, which had names like 'blackcurrant leaf and sticks', and 'rosehip and herring'. I continued to scour the box for anything that might be related to conventional tea. English Breakfast seemed to be the best fit for my predicament, even if the tea bag looked to be filled with the soot scraped from the top of burnt toast.

A short while later the waiter returned with a small metal pot of warm

water and half a lemon in a netting bag. Close to tears, I asked if they had any milk. Again, I was met by confused looks: perhaps the waiter thought I had completely changed my mind about which beverage I wanted. I explained it was for the tea. The waiter took my word for it and said that they didn't have any milk. I tried not to imagine what they were using in the kitchens to make all the batter needed for the huge mounds of pancakes being devoured around me. I also did a quick mental recap on how the process of dairy farming works, to see if there was something obvious I had forgotten. They did, the waiter ventured, have something called half and half. I decided to take my chances, as perhaps half of it would be milk.

The warm water did its best to leach some of the dark colouring from the ash-like substance in the tea bag. The tea bag, though, failed to swell up in that jolly steam-filled way and float to the top of the cup. It dropped forlornly to the bottom instead, as if wounded. Driven on by an almost pathological tea craving, I removed it and added a dash of the half and half, creating a dark brown and greasy mixture, similar to that obtained when washing out a roasting tin after a piece of beef has become stuck to the bottom.

The 'tea' was wet.

The next morning I brought down my own tea bags, and asked for 'very hot water' and some half and half.

The next morning I settled for coffee.

Learning to Love Tea

It's a beguiling idea to think that tea drinking is an innate skill that we are born with. It therefore comes as a bit of a surprise to find that we actually have to learn to drink tea. Just as a child learns to crawl, walk, ride a bike or open those little cartons of juice without squirting it all over themselves, so we all have to learn to drink tea. Here is Wifey, to explain how she developed her craving for the hallowed stuff.

The Importance of Mrs Brown

I was raised in a household where coffee was the drink of choice. Tea was reserved for having with the occasional meal, like a greasy fry-up, or with toast at breakfast-time. When I left home at the tender age of eighteen to become a nurse, I was innocent of its importance in the outside world.

The place I chose to do my training was a very traditional hospital on the outskirts of Belfast. It was run with rods of iron by matrons in starched uniforms, and consultants who were seen, but definitely not spoken to by lowly student nurses. My first placement was in a ward run by as old school a sister as you could ever come across. On my first day she took me aside to tell me that my role for the next six weeks would be to ensure the tidiness and cleanliness of the place, to test urine and to make beds. In that order. To this day, when I make a bed I cringe at the memory of how I was accused of 'slovenly placement of pillows', and carefully arrange them with the open end facing away from the door.

This is where Mrs Brown comes into the story. Patients were not allowed to think of the possibility that staff were actually human beings, who would need to have breaks and possibly a sit down every now and then. This presented a problem, as staff could not possibly go to the ward staffroom without the permission of Sister, at the exact time she had decided it was appropriate for you to do so. Sister, for all her gruff manner, was a fair woman, and she saw it as one of her duties that everyone had an adequate tea intake during the day, whether they liked the stuff or not. So in order to get people into the staffroom for their allocation of tea, they were called to see Mrs Brown. She was treated with reverence. The patients knew that when she called, she could not be kept waiting, despite what their needs were. They never even questioned who Mrs Brown was, despite the fact that this was a male ward.

The tea was made by senior members of staff, who knew how Sister liked it, and this was the way that everyone had it. It was made in a huge pot, with at least five or six heaped teaspoons of special, nameless NHS tea, and wasn't right unless it was thick enough for the spoon to stand upright in the cup. Alternatives, such as increasing or decreasing the amount of sugar or milk in one's cup, were tolerated, although it was accepted that those who drank tea the same way as Sister were most likely to get a favourable report at the end of the placement.

My first week there I hated Mrs Brown, and I had to wonder if nursing was really the career for me. After the second week I began to get used to the taste, found that Sister wasn't really so bad, and the ward really did need to be kept spotless. By the end of my six weeks I couldn't properly function unless I'd been to see Mrs Brown. In short, I'd been turned into a tea addict.

Later in my training I began to appreciate the other skills of Mrs Brown. She made a regular appearance in the ward for the patients at the end of visiting time in the evenings. This was seen as a bedtime treat, and a sign that patients were expected to settle down for the night in time for the arrival of the night staff, who despised patients being awake and talking to them. Mrs Brown also made special appearances in times of bad news. Patients quickly learnt that if they were offered a cup of tea outside normal hours, then they were about to be told something serious. And if their relatives were offered a cup of tea, well, they should make sure all their affairs were in order as quickly as possible.

These days, of course, wards have water coolers and students drink whatever they like, often while having a

chat with the patients about how drunk they were the night before (sometimes even with their arms folded). I do wonder what Mrs Brown would have thought of it all, and whether the place isn't quite so spotlessly clean as it was in her day. Not that it's just the NHS which has been changed by the demise of Mrs Brown. All aspects of society are changing, and not necessarily for the better. There are often surveys done about how difficult it is to get a hold of a good builder or plumber, while avoiding the 'cowboys'. I don't remember these problems years ago when builders where famous for their tea with milk, two sugars and a nice Digestive.

But back to the tea. After years of visiting Mrs Brown my taste buds became used to it and now I can't drink anything else. I've tried the herbal teas and the fruit teas and the Earl Greys, but I can't get on with any of them. They just don't have the kick that I now depend on. To me Earl Grey tastes like tea made in a cup that's been washed with far too much washing-up liquid, and then not properly rinsed. I want to tip it into a clean cup and try again. In fact, I've tried this. It didn't work. I've experimented with herbal teas on and off over the years, but they just don't do it for me. When I was pregnant I was told by my sister to drink raspberry leaf tea, as this would help during labour. I really wanted to like it, but it just made me want to vomit. I gave up after about a week and have now had two boys without its help. I would like to like these exotic teas, much in the same way that I would like to like olives, but I don't.

So I've given up on the tea experimentation. I'll happily change brands of standard tea, and experiment with different types of tea bags, but that's as far as it goes.

Sorry.

Projected Tea Enjoyment

Of course, we mostly learn how to drink tea from our parents, and this results in a quite peculiar and universal phenomenon, that of 'projected tea enjoyment'. In this, the tea drinker imagines that everybody else on the planet likes tea made just the way they like it.

In a well-adjusted family most members enjoy their tea made in the same way: same strength, same temperature, same amount of milk and so forth. This shared family 'tea policy' is most often seen in families that use a teapot. When there is a difference of opinion between parents one or other usually wins out, and the other gradually learns to drink their tea differently. This very act of capitulation only fuels our idea that everyone not only *could* be made to drink tea as we like it but *should* drink tea as we like it. There are many common consequences of this:

 People don't bother asking how you like your tea, assuming you'll drink whatever they give you with relish.

 They do ask you how you like your tea but then totally ignore anything you tell them, thinking that you're bound to enjoy their tea better.

 **They ask you and then violently disagree**, pointing out all the reasons why you are wrong and misguided.

 They try to make it as you have requested but get it all wrong, either maliciously or through ineptitude.

They tell you to make your own tea, not from compassion but because they can't stand to make it in the degenerate way you have suggested.

This explains why you rarely get a nice cup of tea when visiting other people. Of course, it is easy to endear yourself to your host simply by uttering the line, 'That's the best cup of tea I've had in ages', preceded by a sort of gasped '*Ahhhh*' for maximum effect. Your congratulations will bolster your host's already firmly held belief that they do in fact make the best cup of tea on the planet. If you have been sufficiently fawning they might even be moved to get out their really good biscuits.

Our Tea Policy

Well, the thing about tea is that everyone just drinks it
the way they like it. Generally, we make it in mugs, one
tea bag – PG Pyramids – for every two mugs. Put the hot
water in first, then give it a bit of a stir before adding the
milk. Simple. Oh and we don't add sugar. If you drink
any other sort of tea, that's fine. If you put the milk in
with the bag first, that's OK too. Just so long as you
know that it's wrong. Sugar is good too, especially if
you're a builder. Occasionally we use a pot, when we can
be bothered. That's all we have to say on the subject.
Cheers.

 # Tea Bags

The One Per Cup Misunderstanding

A few years ago, while in the employment of a large company, I found myself in the kitchen making a couple of mugs of tea for a colleague and myself. As I did so the company handyman watched me. A chap in his mid-sixties, he was replacing a fluorescent tube, I believe. For making two mugs of tea one bag is of course more than sufficient, yet as I dunked the bag into the second mug I heard him say, 'I've seen everything now! Two mugs with one bag.'

Despite living through World War Two, seeing mankind take their first steps on the moon and the everyday medical miracles of organ trans-plants, the most startling thing the handyman had witnessed in his life was the sight of me making two mugs of tea with one tea bag. I was sorely tempted to deliver a caustic remark. However, as he was a fairly elderly chap and on top of a ladder I thought better of it. His mistake, though, is all too common. Those used to using tea bags straight in a cup or mug often lose sight of the tea bag's original intended purpose.

Technology

The tea bag was introduced as a miraculous labour-saving device to a nation that for nearly three hundred years had made tea from loose leaves brewed in a pot. Although this produces a lovely cuppa, it is a slight chore getting shot of the used tea leaves. The traditional method was to swill some water inside the teapot, wander into the back garden and eject the lot under the roses. Obviously this is a problem for those who live in flats. Those without rose bushes in their gardens also have to improvise. Even those with rose bushes don't always want to see a heap of gently decomposing tea leaves underneath them. There is the option of chucking the whole lot down the sink, but eventually this will probably block it up. It's also a bit of an unnecessary burden on the poor old water works.

The real problem with the used tea leaves in the pot is that it's one more hurdle to jump before you have your much-needed cup of tea. To some it may be part of the ritual, but none the less it is a fairly irksome task. So let's cast our minds back to the 1960s. The Americans were planning on sending a man to the moon and inventing lots of things along the way. The very least the British could do was come up with some way of streamlining their tea-making process. This would also free up invaluable time that could be put to good use, inventing stuff for the 1970s like flared jeans and Raleigh Choppers. The stage was set.

Enter the tea bag, or rather re-enter the tea bag.

At the turn of the twentieth century, the American tea importer Thomas Sullivan sent out some samples of his tea in protective silk bags. His somewhat unorthodox customers assumed that rather than opening up the small sachets (as Sullivan intended), they should just throw the whole thing into their pots. It's ironic that that most British of items, the tea bag, was invented by accident through the actions of some well-meaning but mostly clueless Americans. The tea bag was refined again in America during the 1920s and eventually would be made from paper.

I receive a lot of correspondence on the technicalities of tea brewing, mainly from those who wish to justify their personal tea policies through some form of scientific deduction. If they can show that there is a scientific advantage to their chosen methods then their tea policy will have to be accepted as the one true way, or at the very least an aspect of it. From time to time a popular science story occurs in the media about an aspect of tea and biscuits and this just fans the flames. So don't be scared if you see the word 'molecular' in the next paragraph, it's unavoidable.

The tea used in these early tea bags was intended for pot brewing, and as such could release its flavour, aroma and colour at a gentle and restrained pace. People were used to waiting for the tea to 'mash' for a few minutes and there wasn't any special reason for the tea bag to speed this up. The leaves used were large compared to today: their fibrous structure acted as a natural filter, holding back the bitter, high-molecular-weight tannins (the ones that account for the stewed taste in tea) and allowing the more desirable low-weight tannins to move out of the leaves into the liquid. In other words, the early tea bags produced a cuppa that compared perfectly favourably to that made from loose tea. To ensure that people had a satisfying brew of proper strength, the amount of tea was sufficient to make two cups (the basic assumption being that a bag is sufficient for one person and that person will want two cups of decent tea). Those who adopted tea bags soon found that between two to three bags were ample for a full pot of average size.

As the pace of daily life has increased we have become ever more impatient, and as a result the tea bag has found itself brewing tea outside the teapot. It is commonplace now to make tea in the mug and we don't really care for waiting three or four minutes while it brews. In fact, the modern tea bag needs to do its job in a matter of seconds: the majority of people leave the bag for thirty seconds, while one in four people allow no more than ten seconds. Tea snobs are quick to dismiss tea bags as being filled with 'sweepings'. This is clearly completely ludicrous as 85% of all tea sold in the UK is in the form of bags. The process that produces the 15% loose tea would have to be incredibly wasteful to create enough 'sweepings' to make five times the amount of tea bags. The reality is that much of the tea in bags is now finer to allow for a very quick 'release'. However, this also means the tea is quicker to stew, to the detriment of those using the pot.

Over the years we have seen a pace of innovation in the area of tea bag design so rapid that it is only a few orders of magnitude less than that of washing detergent. After playing about with the contents, manufacturers then began to make the holes or pores in the bags bigger. Then some bags changed shape from square-ish to round and now pyramidal. The format also evolved; now you can get special bags with tags and strings to be whipped out of cups, drawstrings that wring out the bag, and the 'one cup bag', with just enough tea to make one nice cup. Oi! You up the ladder! Did you hear that? If tea bags had been meant for only one cup then why did they have to invent the one cup bag? And what about those little stainless-steel teapots, the ones you get at motorway service stations that empty the tea all over the table? They only have one bag in them, yet do they not contain about two and a half cups of tea? I rest my case.

All of this bag technology could have presented the rose bushes which had acquired a taste for a couple of pots of tea a day with quite a problem. Most of the used tea bags were finding their way straight into the rubbish bin, ultimately to be buried in landfills. Not a very dignified end for all those little leaf tips that started life under the sunshine of an Indian or African sky. However, in recent times it has dawned upon most of us that we need to take a bit of individual responsibility for our environment, and home composting is a great way of helping out. Used tea bags make excellent compost and not only do the roses benefit but so does the rest of the garden, particularly the marrows and courgettes. One of the most relaxing ways to pass a warm summer's afternoon is to sit in the garden, admiring your crop of Cucurbitaceae flourishing on composted tea bags. While drinking a mug of tea and munching on a biscuit, of course.

Sugar

Tea tastes bitter, and many tea drinkers when starting out take theirs with a spoonful of sugar to offset this taste. As we get older our tastes change and we start to enjoy flavours such as tea, beer, olives and tonic water. However, we still don't enjoy those dreadful local speciality liquors you get given on holiday in the Alps, the ones that taste like a solution of paracetamol filtered through old carpet soaked in petrol. The sugar in tea also provides a little energy lift that can be quite welcome. I took sugar in my tea right up to going to university. However, once there I quickly gave it up. This wasn't because I wanted to establish my sophisticated adult credentials, but because my cupboard in the shared kitchen was so tiny I couldn't fit a bag of sugar in it. That and the fact I was totally broke.

But perhaps the most meaningful part of giving up sugar is the fact that it is one less thing to bother with when making tea. Having grown used to this extra level of convenience, most non-sugar people find it galling to have to dig some out for those who still require it. They are often still quite smug about the ten days' self-sacrifice they had to endure while giving up, and are keen for others to share that pain. Their agenda now is to get everybody else to stop taking sugar, and they have a number of well-known approaches when making tea for a sugar user:

 **Deny the sugar-user direct access to the sugar bowl**, insisting that they put it in and then deliberate give less sugar than requested. The expectation is that rather than complain about the lack of sweetness, the sugar person will declare that this is the nicest cup of tea they have ever had, and enquire how it was made so extra especially nice.

 **Dig out a really ancient bag of sugar which has a few ounces left at the bottom.** Here one can find all the accumulated brown and yellow lumps where people have been forced to stick their damp tea-spoons in, and possibly the odd toast crumb. The bag itself has begun to yellow with age, and where one would normally expect to see a bar-code there is a competition to win some 45r.p.m. vinyl singles. There may even be grubby marks where it has become embroiled in some post-bicycle-chain-mending hand-cleansing. Of course, the hardened sugar user will be undeterred and somehow retrieve pristine spoonfuls.

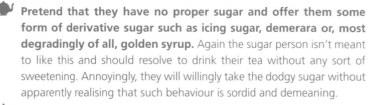

Pretend that they don't have any sugar at all in the house, and force the sugar person to have it without. Of course, they won't like this at all but the ex-sugar person will know that it is in fact good for them both physically and mentally. For good measure they'll probably want to insist that the sugar person has a second cup.

Pretend that they have no proper sugar and offer them some form of derivative sugar such as icing sugar, demerara or, most degradingly of all, golden syrup. Again the sugar person isn't meant to like this and should resolve to drink their tea without any sort of sweetening. Annoyingly, they will willingly take the dodgy sugar without apparently realising that such behaviour is sordid and demeaning.

Genuinely not have any sugar in the house, and derive some sort of sick pleasure from watching the poor sugar user suffer as they are forced to drink 'proper' tea.

The ultimate cruelty: give them some form of artificial sweetener, because the non-sugar user is also a recovering sugar addict and has managed to persuade themself that they actually enjoy the taste of saccharine. Only now they've become hooked on the sweeteners, and are starting to use more and more as they don't seem to be quite as sweet as they once were. Perhaps they can lure the sugar user into their twisted world where they too will have to carry their own personal supply of sweeteners in their jacket pocket. Oh yes, they know only too well what can happen if they're deprived of their tablets and forced to take up the offer of the sugar bowl. You might as well give a bottle of vodka to a recovering alcoholic.

There are times in life when we are not too choosy about our tea. At such times even the most out-of-kilter brew can become divine nectar. Anything handed out by the emergency services tends to be simultaneously both of these opposites and often contains a good helping of sugar.

 # Teapots

A Potted History

The Chinese invented tea, and probably about twenty minutes later the teapot to make some in. There are teapots that date back to the early Ming dynasty, which is nice as that is most people's favourite dynasty. These earliest pots were fairly selfish affairs as you were meant to drink the tea directly from the spout. (Mind you, how many of us can honestly say that we haven't done that ourselves at times?) Teapots as we know them were really a seventeenth-century European invention, most likely based directly on the Islamic coffee pots which were already well known in the coffee houses of Europe's great cities. Early models were ropey old affairs due to the poor quality of ceramics used to make them. In fact, one early design even featured a replaceable spout as they broke so often.

So it was back to China to get some proper porcelain ones made to European specifications. The East India Company, who ran the tea business back then, commissioned teapots directly from Chinese artisans. These teapots were incredibly expensive, having been brought halfway round the world in a trip that could take a total of three years there and back. As such, they were as much a status symbol of the well to do as they were a functional object. But the desire by the middle classes to take part in the elite and fashionable ritual of afternoon tea fuelled a huge new market for teapots, and European alternatives to porcelain began to appear.

It's ironic that today most of the upper classes have had to turn their stately homes in to tea rooms, their gardens into car parks and their stables into public conveniences in order to attract the working classes into their estates. If they also laid on bingo and chicken in a basket, I'm sure they'd soon be back in the lap of luxury.

Now in the twenty-first century we have 300 years of European teapot tradition and innovation to draw upon. Our teapot heritage runs from Josiah Wedgwood's Creamware, through the many and varied influences on Victorian teapots, to the modernists and the postmodernists. Let's see if we can find one that doesn't pour its contents all over our feet.

Form and Function

The pen and the car: two commodities at opposite ends of the spectrum of costs. A new pen may cost only a matter of pence and yet you get to try it out on a little jotter pad. You can write your name, do some squiggles or your favourite doodle before deciding whether to splash out 70 pence on it. Equally, when buying a car, even a bottom-of-the-range model, you get to take it out for a test drive. You might keep it only a year or two, but you still get to make your choice safe in the knowledge that at least it went OK the day you bought it.

So why don't you get to do the same with teapots?

There are two primary mission objectives that any teapot should fulfil: holding enough tea and being able to get it into your cup without spilling it everywhere. A teapot test-drive zone in your local department store would be a boon to those in need of a new pot. Health and Safety might not like people boiling kettles, so cold tea would need to be used. No doubt it would have a slightly different viscosity to proper hot tea which could affect the results, but let's be realistic and not set our sights unattainably high.

No, I've changed my mind. Let's aim high. One could sign a disclaimer, indemnifying the store from your possible self-harm. Then you could enter a special teapot-testing cubicle with little bulletproof Plexiglas view ports, through which your loved ones could look on. Alternatively, you could take out a short-term insurance policy covering the store against possible breakage, carpet staining and total catastrophic destruction of their teapot-testing cubicles. It could also cover you against scalds, tea-stained clothes and trench foot.

Obviously one is after a good clean pouring action which starts and stops without any nasty surprises. The ability to pour well is prized above all else, including capacity, as it's no good how much your pot can hold if it then pours most of it over your feet and table. There should be no dribbling or trickling. Spout pressure should not drop away too prohibitively towards the last cups. Finally, the pot should feel balanced and pouring from it should be comfortable no matter how full it is.

Having said all that, the capacity issue cannot be glossed over and there really is only one way to test it: with a row of mugs or cups which closely match or, better still, replicate your domestic drinking vessel set-up. It's going to be easier if you have matching sets and a bit more tricky if you have to simulate a variety of personal mugs and cups. Perhaps you could select them from a laminated illustrated catalogue, via a code number: the test-zone personnel could then fetch them from a large system of racks using little trays. The mugs should all be glazed white, possibly with those little black and yellow quarter-circle thingies that crash-test dummies have all over them, placed at strategic points. If you are intending to use tea bags then it's imperative that you use your own brand as they will no doubt have their own volumetric signature when they swell up.

When using leaf tea the shape of the pot becomes even more crucial. Clearly the tea brewing is going to be affected by the convection currents in your pot, even after you've given it a good stir. No, the real issue with pot shape is spout clogging. The placing of the spout, its width, taper and extra moulded-in paraphernalia to catch the leaves all contribute. The shape of some pots can also cause annoying cubby holes in which limescale and wayward tea leaves can congregate. They will hide here and then spring out at you when you least expect it, black and scaly or bleached and insipid.

The next most important issue is lid retention. Even some of the most potentially nice pots can suffer from premature lid loss right in the middle of a good pour. This can be acutely embarrassing for all concerned. It's a great shame as there really is no excuse for it. It can even lead to some pots becoming virtual recluses, living out their days at the back of kitchen cupboards.

Apart from a nice comfy handle and a good stable 'footprint', that's most of the practical considerations out of the way. Now you are free to make purely aesthetic decisions such as will it go with the curtains and does it complement your tea service. But if you find a teapot that really does deliver in the vital areas I've outlined then it might be easier just to get new curtains and redecorate the house around it.

🫖 **Work Tea Making**

When The Tea Bags Run Out

There are certain events that can have a dramatic impact on productivity in the modern office environment, effectively bringing any useful work to a standstill. Power cuts, fire drills, World Cup matches and Wimbledon fortnight can all be crippling, but none is as damaging as running out of tea bags. A form of mild mass-hysteria soon sets in, with employees wandering aimlessly with empty mugs, moaning bitterly about the lack of tea.

An all too common mistake in an office is to put the most junior member of staff in charge of the task of ordering stationery and kitchen supplies. An even bigger error is to put the visiting foreign work experience student in charge. Not only will their youth and inexperience count against them but their cultural background will make them unaware of the gravity and responsibility of keeping a good stock of tea bags. Even if such matters are made plain to them they may actually not drink tea (it *is* possible) and thus be completely unaware of tea bag levels and any impending 'no tea bag' calamities.

A responsible managing director will take steps to ensure that the company places somebody trustworthy in charge of tea bags, such as the lady in accounts who does the payroll. Often these unsung heroes can stave off a crisis situation by popping to the local shop to get a box of tea bags when supplies are low. Such occasions are when their spreadsheet model of tea bag consumption has been thrown into disarray by a late delivery of the catering-size sacks of tea bags from the suppliers, or a surge in tea drinking due to a particularly dull workload.

Tea Notation

There are various things in this world of ours which require some form of notation to describe their composition or make-up. For example, the chemical notation for sodium bicarbonate, a common raising agent in biscuits, is:

$$NaHCO_3$$

From this we learn that there is one atom of sodium, one of hydrogen, one of carbon and three of oxygen per molecule of sodium bicarbonate. You might have thought that noting how people take their tea would be a much simpler task than recording the chemical composition of compounds. Well, it's not.

Most people will hastily invent a drinks notation on the spot when making tea for a group of people. A typical approach might be 'T' for tea and 'C' for coffee. Of course, the next most important fact to note is sugar, and this is simply dealt with by the addition of a number. 'T2' is thus not a film staring Arnold Schwarzenegger, but tea with two sugars. Just as you think you have that part under control, somebody pipes up that they like a level, not heaped, teaspoon. Somebody else adds that they actually just like half a level teaspoonful, unless it's coffee, when they like one heaped.

Then there are those who take their drinks black, which being the exception to the rule is denoted by a 'B'. However, those who take it with milk will typically like it with 'a dash', 'normal' (by far the most difficult one to get right) or 'milky', so we might get a third column with 'B', 'D', or 'M' in it. Not that this is the end of it: somebody always wants something odd like Earl Grey, for which you'll need to write down 'Earl Grey' in full. By rights this should be it, but it's not. Some like it weak, some strong, some 'normal' again. So you may need a fourth column with 'W' and 'S' in it.

Surely we must be done by now? Well, normally, yes, at this point good manners should prevail and people should drink whatever is put in front of them. However, there may also be the occasional person who will insist that you track down their personal mug. This might require you to take a description or even possibly a small sketch of the intended mug with you. In extreme cases, you may be forced to do their dirty work and retrieve it for them from the dishwasher, or worse still the sales department.

Still, armed with a semi-accurate list of people's preferences, you can not only get the drinks in, but might gain insight into their personalities. For instance:

T3MW	–	Immature
T	–	Very normal
T1L	–	Normal sugar user
Earl Grey 0.5 B Lemon Peter Rabbit Mug	–	Very annoying
CBS Large Mug	–	Party animal / New parent

This provides a welcome bit of light relief as making drinks for a dozen or more people is going to keep you in the kitchen for the next ten minutes of your life. Effectively this is like taking a small fire-safety course: by the time you make it out of there, boredom will have driven you to read the instructions on the fire extinguisher and the fire blanket, and you'll also know where to congregate in case of an emergency. You may also be wondering why the egg tray in the fridge door has managed to collect some small deposits of a semi-solid, yellow, waxy substance despite never seeing an egg in its entire existence.

Studying people's preferences can also prove useful for gauging who is going to object to whatever they are given. See if you can spot the troublemaker from the list above. You may have thought it was the Earl Grey drinker, but they will be quite happy with what you give them as it all tastes the same regardless of what you do to it. It's actually the first one, who will claim that there isn't enough sugar in it, and they are probably right, aren't they?

Kettle Etiquette

We tend to think that our values as a society are being constantly eroded. The things that we value, such as respect for others and orderly behaviour, seem to be put under increasing strain in our overcrowded and busy world. However, queuing for things in an orderly way is something that the British have always taken pride in. In fact, one of the most repugnant social crimes of all is queue jumping. Anyone committing this heinous act is subjected to withering stares and even the occasional indirect jibe, discussed between two law-abiding queue members and designed to be overheard by the queue jumper.

The imported American idea of a 'water cooler culture' in the UK is of course a falsehood. We drink tea, not little paper cups of water, even if the weather is hot. All the discussion on the latest and greatest reality TV show takes place over the electric kettle, in the office kitchen. The water cooler, if one exists, is actually regarded with a degree of suspicion and mistrust. Most people don't like to be seen using it as somebody is obviously having a joke at our expense, and making the company pay for cold water when the taps are full of it.

As such, the office kettle is the place where our social skills are challenged to the limit as we gather round it and struggle not to disgrace ourselves. When to fill the kettle and when to use the boiled water are matters on which our peers will judge us, and nobody likes a queue jumper. Here are some guidelines that you might care to memorise:

 Social ranking. Everybody is an equal in the sight of the kettle. Company directors and their guests enjoy no special privileges, waiting their turn along with everybody else.

 The water in the kettle should only be boiled once, as repeated boiling drives off the dissolved oxygen that is considered essential for good tea. It is therefore better to use any boiled water left in the kettle than to add more cold and boil it again.

 Big jobs. If somebody is making tea for a large number of people, say in excess of three, then they will require exclusive use of the kettle and probably a time-consuming full boil from cold. Their right to do this should be respected. However, if there is enough freshly boiled water in the kettle to meet the needs of the people directly behind them in the queue, then it should be offered to them.

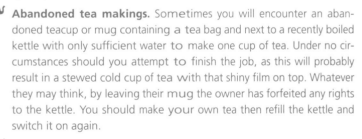 **Abandoned tea makings.** Sometimes you will encounter an abandoned teacup or mug containing a tea bag and next to a recently boiled kettle with only sufficient water to make one cup of tea. Under no circumstances should you attempt to finish the job, as this will probably result in a stewed cold cup of tea with that shiny film on top. Whatever they may think, by leaving their mug the owner has forfeited any rights to the kettle. You should make your own tea then refill the kettle and switch it on again.

Catastrophic kettle failure. Any technical problems with a kettle, such as a blown fuse or dead element, should be immediately notified to the correct authorities (usually the lady in accounts). A yellow Post-It note with the word 'Dead' written on it should be affixed to the kettle. A company email memo should be circulated advising of the crisis and the actions that are being taken to remedy it. It is better that people learn of these things first hand rather than via ugly rumours.

 **Mugs**

Mug Menagerie

The average workplace kitchen has five distinct forms of drinking vessel, intended for deployment with hot beverages, such as soup, hot chocolate, coffee and of course tea:

 Proper plain white cups and saucers that get used in meetings with visitors.

Generic mugs that are slightly oddly shaped, typically no more than six, that were bought from a department store as the cheapest thing they had. These are intended for everybody's use. Unfortunately the mugs were seconds – that's why they were cheap – and those that still have handles compensate with strange glazed warts.

A seemingly unlimited supply of some form of promotional mug, which somebody in marketing had made to give away as freebies. If one of these ever breaks then somebody can always pop down to the store cupboard and get another box of fifty. Such mugs are intrinsically embarrassing as they often commemorate a hopelessly out of date or discontinued product or perhaps a marketing campaign that was widely accepted to be the most expensive and least effective yet. It's not uncommon for the more subversive employees to use these mugs in some form of obtuse political statement. (They are often the reason why the lady from accounts had to go out and buy the nice set of cups and saucers for meetings with visitors.)

Samples. Hiding among the personal mugs is a small community of one-off samples that were made for the people in marketing. These feature horrendous colour schemes, defunct logos, and incorrect post-codes and telephone numbers.

 Personal mugs. These are brought in by the employees themselves and are characterised by the fact that they are meant to be repellent to other people.

Personal Mugs Explained

If an Englishman's home is his castle, then his mug is what he drinks his tea out of. This also applies to other nations and to the ladies. So it's little wonder that most of us go off the deep end when somebody uses our personal mug. They might as well complete the job by pinching our tooth-brush and putting on our underwear.

There are a number of reasons why people turn to the loathsome crim-inal activity that is mug theft. The most common excuse is that there are no clean mugs. This is a malaise that, perversely, affects kitchens that have a dishwasher, leading to a climate of diminished social responsibility in which people simply don't bother to clean their mugs. Instead, huge filthy colonies build up on work surfaces: occasionally these are put in the dishwasher, which is able to warehouse vast quantities. As most people don't know how to use the dishwasher, or consider themselves to have insufficient authority to switch it on, clean mugs quickly become scarce. People may even resort to using the warty no-handle mug.

Driven by desperation, the unscrupulous mug thief turns to what is obviously somebody's personal mug. They justify their actions by reasoning that it is almost lunchtime and that person hasn't used their mug so far today so maybe they have become disaffected with it or simply abandoned it. The people most at risk here are those who have been out of the office for the morning, anybody off sick or those on holiday. It's not uncommon to return from a long weekend to find that your mug has gone missing, to say nothing of your swivel chair and computer keyboard.

Of course, there is always the possibility that your mug isn't languishing on the culprit's desk alongside your keyboard but has in fact found its way into the dishwasher. Not only that, but uncharacteristically this has been switched on, thus presenting you with three choices:

 Patiently wait the forty-five minutes it takes for the dishwasher to remove the graphics or design from the outside of your mug and identifies it as yours (how they manage to do this using hot water and a bit of soap is a wonder of the modern world).

 Open up the dishwasher and take your life in your hands as you rummage around in a scalding-hot hell of mugs and partially cleaned bowls of tomato soup.

 Use the warty no-handle mug. You may have to remove eight months' worth of dust from the bottom of it. In some situations it may have gone completely native and be sporting a small bunch of flowers, helping to brighten up the place. Or maybe it's languishing inside the fridge door half full of curry sauce.

NEW STARTERS

There is nothing more embarrassing than having to go up to some-body who has only just started working in the office and make a big scene to claim back your mug. Watching them bolt down a scalding-hot cuppa as you stand there, tea bag in hand, can create an unpleasant atmosphere. This can be compounded if, as a temporary transfer from one of your European offices, English is not their native tongue, and due to your heightened emotional state, you are using language they didn't learn on their two-week refresher course. Why the person who shows them around the department on their first day forgot to brief them on which mugs they are allowed to use is anybody's guess. New starters will often feel guilty about their wrongdoings and to atone for their sins will use the warty no-handle mug until their request for a transfer comes through.

Personal Mug Types

 Twee. Anything with flowers, bunnies, kittens, puppies, pictures of cot-tages or those flat-headed teddies with the line down the middle of their face.

 Pottery class. Lopsided and ugly dark blue monstrosities that weigh as much as a small family car.

 Giant. Enormous mugs about the size of a small saucepan, usually with something written on the side about how much caffeine this person requires just to function. Never follow this person into the kitchen, as they might have to boil two kettlefuls before they are done.

Rustic. These look like they have been made from reformed roof tiles, plant pots or the same stuff that they use to make those brown glazed pipes at the bottom of manholes.

Impractical. Novelty-shaped mugs might seem like a terrific Christmas-present idea to some, but to the poor recipient they provide weeks of

unsatisfactory tea drinking. Having a ceramic mouse looking at you from the depths of your tea or a mug handle in the shape of an ear is simply annoying. Not only that, but these embellishments collect limescale and grime. Sometimes the dishwasher will do you a favour and smash it up. Either that or it will spontaneously fracture or topple over, thereby bringing its sad existence to an end.

 Pint glass. There is always somebody who insists on drinking their tea out of a pint glass. As a general rule, it simply isn't worth engaging these people in conversation.

 Rude. Something fairly crude and usually belonging to one of the girls in telesales. This mug is very successful at keeping mug thieves at bay. Most people don't have the bottle to be seen drinking out of something that says 'World's Greatest Lover' or is shaped like a part of the body.

 Tall, thin mugs. People who use these like to imagine that really they are drinking from fine bone china. Well, they're not.

 Obviously yours. Something with your name, your face, your children or your pet on it.

 Dull. A promotional mug given to you by one of your suppliers, like 'Dreary and Wett, suppliers of long bits of wire with little lumps at the end'. Typically there will be a very dull logo which looks just like a square, or possibly a circle.

Tragic. The promotional mug for the last company that you worked for, which you still use even though they made you redundant.

Wifey says

That's all very well, Nicey, but why do we insist on keeping all our old promotional work mugs from years ago at the back of the cupboard? All they do is collect dust, and no matter how many people turn up for tea we would never be bold enough to get them out. It's ridiculous! Let's get our house mug situation sorted out before we start insulting people's work mugs!

Filthy Mugs

As we have seen, most personal mugs are designed to repel others. However, this will not always be enough of a deterrent on its own.

Some people resort to using filth in the war against mug crime. By giving their mugs little more than a cursory rinse under the cold tap, a thick laminated crust of brown muck can be created inside the mug. Those who prey on unattached clean mugs are naturally put off by this, as is virtually any creature higher up the food chain than a woodlouse. The people who have been driven to plumb such depths of mug hygiene – generally men – actually seem to enjoy drinking tea from these filthy vessels. The long-term health consequences are unknown but their chances of starting an office romance are almost zero.

Dark Mugs

In the headlong rush to create ever more varieties of mug, there is one problem that occurs time and time again: dark mugs. Anything finished with navy-blue, bottle-green or even black glazes simply doesn't make good tea. The contents of the mug will always appear weak and pallid, as if deficient in tea and milk, even when they are not. Nevertheless, the bewildered tea drinker will keep dunking their tea bag and adding milk until their brew takes on the appearance of tea. By now they have completely ruined their cuppa, unless they like very strong, very milky tea, of course.

Even if the tea drinker finds the mental strength to ignore the evil dark mug mind games, their tea will still look weak and wishy-washy, causing them background levels of anguish.

Some
Biscuits

 Biscuits

It is important to celebrate all that biscuits have achieved throughout the course of history and certainly since the 1970s. We should also look forward to a time when advanced, satisfying and tasty biscuits are being routinely eaten by pioneering tea drinkers in space, or in colonies on the distant moons of the great gas giant planets, or possibly even in France.

How to Taste Biscuits

At times the sheer number and variety of biscuits in the world can seem overwhelming and daunting. Even the small selection that we have assembled for this book may contain some that are new or unfamiliar to you.

Be not afraid.

Tasting biscuits at a professional level, you might think, requires great discipline and skill. Perhaps a point system that assesses crunch, taste, size, dunking suitability, pack design, fruit content, chocolate quality and so on could be devised. But would this really tell us anything? No, not really.

The best approach I have found is to eat the first one quite slowly, then just steam into the rest, washing them down with lots of tea. You'll soon get the measure of them and, as you can imagine, this technique requires virtually no skill and a complete lack of discipline. You can also tell yourself that you are using a holistic approach, even if you didn't really have any sort of approach in mind.

For the sake of thoroughness, you might want to see off a whole packet to yourself. Through this you'll learn exactly how filling an entire pack is and be better able to make important quantitative buying decisions should you decide to share the next pack with family and friends. You'll run the risk of being seen as a fairly tight and selfish individual but that's a small price to pay for disciplined rigour.

Let's face it, if you look at wine tasting as a comparable sort of thing then there isn't much to fear. I've lost count of the amount of times I've heard a wine critic describe a red wine as being full of 'lots of red fruits'. Well, yes, that's how they make it. Perhaps they might want to follow that up with 'It's a liquid at room temperature' and some other obvious statement like 'Gravity stops it coming out of the top of the bottle by itself'. Or how about 'It goes great with a meal or can be enjoyed by itself'? Well, yes, that's because it's a drink. That's what they're for.

How to Buy Biscuits

Supermarkets, corner shops, petrol stations and newsagents' are all good places to view and buy biscuits. Of course, none of these establishments offer tasting, or as the French call it '*degustation*', so you have to buy before you can try. Sometimes you will encounter biscuits in 'touristy' type shops that you'll naturally view with a healthy scepticism, and you'd be right to. Many probably have more in common with 'olde-worlde' surroundings than just the quaint pictures of cottages on the box. Always check the best-before dates to see if they were baked in living memory. If the box is covered in Olde English writing make sure it wasn't baked in Olde England.

If you are in one of those 'buy anything for a pound' shops then you'll find the biscuits between the giant ceramic Dalmatians and the commemorative disbanded boy band full-length mirrors. This might be a good place to buy a novelty biscuit tin, in the shape of a large frog or teddy bear, if that's the bag you're into.

When buying biscuits, by all means pick up the packets to examine them. The most obvious thing you can learn from this are the actual dimensions of the biscuits, which often bear little correlation with the picture on the pack. You might even go as far as measuring them with a little tape measure to see if the unopened packs will fit in your tins. (A tip for married men: it's best not to have your wife present if you decide to measure biscuits in public.)

You may wish to read the product description and then tally this up against the ingredients, to see if these 'lemony' biscuits have ever seen a real lemon. Another useful guide is that ingredients are listed in descending order of mass. So any ingredients listed after the salt and raising agents are present only in trace element amounts. For example, this is not where you want to find the raisins.

Carry your biscuits carefully to the checkout to avoid damaging them. If using a basket or trolley, place your biscuits safely in the bottom. If you are also buying frozen poultry, try not to drop this on your biscuits from a great height. Don't attempt to fold any boxes or packs in half, and don't use long packs to act out any of the light-sabre scenes from *Star Wars*.

It's also a good idea to form a strategy for dealing with BOGOF (buy one get one free) and multi-buy savers. These are designed to strip away any free will you thought you had and get you to buy something else. A good strategy is to simply give in to their mind games and buy a big bunch of whatever it is they think you should have. You'll be all right, providing you eat them sensibly and not all in one go in the car park.

How to Store Biscuits

Why should you want to store your biscuits? If you have managed to breach their packaging and not eaten them all then the proper storage of your biscuits is a good idea. Not only will it stop them going stale and limp but it may protect against casual and opportunistic theft. Many people take an open biscuit packet as an invitation to help themselves to whichever biscuit treat you may currently be enjoying.

Also, eating biscuits straight from the pack makes it all too obvious to the biscuit thief when you have something new and glamorous in your possession.

In the office, some individuals may be labouring under the illusion that there is a feudal system at work in which biscuits are paid as some form of tithe, to directors and various upper management. Those with a shred of conscience will tend to buy on an annual basis an inappropriate, if well-intentioned pack of biscuits. The biscuits produced will either be too small, too fancy or just too few in number to be a credible offering. The pack or packs will be offered to all and sundry in a flamboyant and public and fashion, while the giver warmly reminds everyone of the last packet of biscuits that they dispensed. The intention is to flood your consciousness with images of you receiving biscuits from them. Absolutely nobody is taken in by this, with the possible exception of the new starter.

Another common misconception is that people who are 'working late' are entitled to lay siege to any biscuits that they can locate on company property. This is wrong for so many reasons it's almost beneath us to go into them. Apologetic yellow notes stuck to your computer screen saying 'Sorry for eating all your biscuits' don't cut it, but a pay rise might go some way to assuaging the pain.

There are two main schools of thought when it comes to biscuit storage. One simply advocates placing the open packs still intact inside the storage vessel. This has the advantage of keeping the documentation that accompanies your biscuits (the pack) close at hand should it become necessary to refer to it. It also allows you to keep a tight hold on your stock levels without having to turf through random piles of biscuits. The second approach is simply to empty the packs straight into your storage vessel. This seemingly haphazard approach is actually a subtle and complex art, which has parallels in such pastimes as flower arranging, the construction of drystone walls and making a really good tossed salad. In fact all those Japanese Zen Buddhist rock gardeners should try arranging Custard Creams, Fruit Shortcakes and Digestives in an old Rover selection tin for an alternative path to enlightenment.

Like it or not, other people will always judge you on the contents of your biscuit tin, and if they are polite they may not even tell you that they are doing so. You'll have nothing to fear from this if your tin is up to scratch. In fact, it might provide the opportunity for a little light-hearted recreational disagreement on the merits of various biscuits.

A really accomplished mixed tin should be pleasing to the eye as well as the palate. Each species of biscuit should contribute to the harmonious whole, and no one type should dominate the others. The overall effect should not be ostentatious nor should it appear austere. If you do feel the need to favour each extreme then you should seriously consider setting aside a second tin for the purpose. That way you can indulge your need for self-denial by having a spartan tin of Thin Arrowroots and Rich Teas, while your friends can enjoy a decent selection of biscuits from your second, public-facing tin. Alternatively you may like to wallow in a sea of thick chocolate-covered excess, leaving your guests to look for the simple pleasures of Fruit Shortcake. Then again, you may simply be a bit stingy, and prefer to hide all your chocolate biscuits.

Strong flavours should be stored separately as the other milder shortcake or Digestive-based biscuits will absorb ginger, fruity, spicy or even coconut flavours, to their detriment. New and radical biscuits such as maple syrup and toffee apple flavour should be quarantined until such times as they are proven safe to mix with other biscuits, though this is seldom the case.

A great many of nature's bounties require a little work before we can reap the rewards. Nature provides fruits, shellfish and nuts with skins and shells that force us to work a little before we feast upon what's inside. Biscuits echo this age-old struggle of hunter-gatherer pitted against nature's harvest. The tough and durable outer wrappers of biscuit packs have evolved to protect their sweet and tasty contents from humidity, sunlight, pests, other biscuits and, of course, us, the consumer. At times it appears that the strongest substance yet devised by mankind isn't titanium or stainless steel but cellophane.

Just as those three little dark holes at the top of a coconut appear to offer some means of access, which actually rarely helps, so the little red strip round a biscuit pack is purely there to mock us. At home there are plenty of ways of cracking open a stubborn pack of biscuits, from a full set of steak knives to that circular saw in the shed. However, in the office environment the hungry biscuit eater may have to improvise when faced with a particularly intractable pack. Some resort to the logical reversal of the packing process, deliberately undoing each seam in succession until access is finally gained. The biscuit packers are expecting just this sort of attack and will have fused both pack ends into laminated shields, in a process licensed to or from the manufacturers of tank armour, I expect.

Typically there follows a short but vicious biting attack on the pack, mostly involving the canine teeth. This is only appropriate for those situations where the biscuits are solely for personal consumption, as there is nothing nastier than being offered biscuits from a pack covered in dribble. The pack can usually defeat such an obvious attack through two simple means: a specially hardened pack seam and high-tension wrapping. This results in the cellophane being pulled so tightly over the biscuits that it proves impossible to nip any part of it between the teeth.

When faced with such an impervious pack most office workers will take the only sensible course of action: seeking out the holder of the office Swiss Army knife. Most often this is the guy who insists on dismantling his computer, window blind and gas-pump chair for no apparent reason. He is also uncharacteristically popular at the Christmas party when all those bottles of Australian Shiraz languishing in drawer bottoms need opening.

Of course, if you really do need to break in to some biscuits then simply straighten out a thin paper clip and push the end into the pack between two biscuits, then move it round in a lateral fashion. Depending on the cellophane, this will often produce an attractive frilly cut in the pack, which is an added bonus. A note of caution: always take care with straightened-out paper clips or you'll have somebody's eye out.

Wrappers ■

It goes without saying, but let's say it: don't keep your biscuit storage vessel in direct sunlight or on top of a radiator, especially if it contains chocolate biscuits. If you insist on doing this then you might want to keep a spoon, barbecue tongs, some straws, a kitchen roll and a pack of wet wipes handy.

Try to layer your biscuits in such a way that all varieties are easily accessible without the need to struggle down to the bottom of the tin, causing unnecessary and unsightly breakages. It may be tempting to arrange your biscuits in stacks: however, this will simply cause you anxiety and upset as eager hands lay waste to your neatly regimented biscuits.

Watch out for hidden biscuits that behave like little man traps, crushing the ends of your fingers in their powerful vice-like grip. Luckily I can't think of any that are like that. Still, no harm in staying alert.

Anybody who routinely kills pot plants will probably not have realised that you need to water them or, alternatively, that they don't need watering three times a day. Biscuits are also extraordinarily sensitive to moisture, and the microclimate of your biscuit tin will need careful attention. Moist biscuits such as the Fig Roll dry out while the other biscuits around them will absorb their moisture. This effectively turns both types of biscuit stale despite using a sealed container. The danger can be lessened by choosing a variety of Fig Roll that has been cut before baking, such as a Jacob's or Crawford's, as the moist fig is less exposed. You should also avoid mixing biscuits and cakes in the same tin for the same reasons.

Finally, don't bury your biscuit tin in the garden, then dig it up twenty-nine years later and expect everything to be fine. They tried that on *Blue Peter* in 1971. When they dug it up in 2000, all the stuff in the tin was badly messed up, having turned into a sort of inky black soup. It wasn't even biscuits in the tin but a copy of the *Radio Times*, a *Blue Peter Annual*, pictures and tapes.

Some Storage Options

A Biscuit Barrel

Designed for the job, a biscuit barrel is the expert's choice: it provides portability and tight seals and maintains confidentiality until such times as it is opened. Most are fitted with a silica-gel insert in the lid, designed to draw the moisture from the air and keep your biscuits crisp and crunchy. A little gold-coloured knob on the top is best, and some of the finest examples are decorated, confusingly, with pictures of fruit.

If you really want to do your biscuit barrel proud then decorate your kitchen with that wallpaper that has little pictures of teapots and coffee pots on it. Or just strip away seven or eight layers of paper and find that somebody already did it for you.

A Tin

A good alternative, especially for those on a budget, or who dislike the effects of the silica-gel thingy. The most important aspect is a sensible lid which fits snugly, yet may easily be removed. The older the tin, the better, as it will have an air of authority to it.

A Plastic Container

This is not an elegant solution, and can trap strong flavours long after the biscuits have been eaten. Given that it can create the impression that you are on some kind of picnic, maybe you can complete the image by drinking your tea from an enamel mug and sitting on your coat on the floor.

A Drawer

Handy if you work in an office but hardly airtight. Take care not to get items of stationery such as staples and paper clips mixed up in your biscuits. It does have the frequent advantage of being lockable.

A Cookie Jar

Placing your biscuits inside something that is meant for cookies or, worse still, has 'Cookies' written on the outside is too traumatic for many. Most right-thinking biscuit eaters will be more than a little irritated by the sheer cultural imperialism of the word 'cookie'. Overall, the British response to cookies is much the same as that of a parent being enlightened by their child on popular music. It's not that we don't like it; we just don't want them to think they invented it.

Glass cookie jars are a particularly bad idea, in much the same way as those ludicrous transparent vinyl bags, briefly popular in the 1980s, which showed pickpockets all they needed to know, as well as letting the whole world view your hairbrush. If your biscuit selection is a bit lacklustre then it will be on show for all to see and may cause you embarrassment which might otherwise have been avoided. The really big ones are also far from portable, limiting their usefulness: you may be forced to abandon your nice sit down to traipse over to where the cookie jar is holding court.

 **Classification**

The Class Struggle

There are broadly speaking three bands into which biscuits fall: entry level, mid-range and luxury. It's useful to be aware of the bands as each is more expensive than the one before, and it might help you to spot a bargain. Another way of viewing it is as a sort of class structure for biscuits, moving from dead common, through middle class to terribly posh.

Here are some approximate guidelines for determining a biscuit's grouping. Exercise these with caution as sometimes you can find mutton dressed as lamb, or equally something swish that has fallen on hard times.

 Entry-Level Biscuits: homogeneous and simple biscuits often in clear cellophane wrappers. They don't mind shacking up and sometimes you can find up to three different types of biscuit sharing the same outer wrapper. Expect nothing more glamorous than a bit of cream filling or some sugar on top. You are likely to find such biscuits at convenience shops, petrol stations and dreary town-centre supermarkets run by companies you thought went to the wall years ago. Unless you are ravenously hungry it's unlikely that you'll eat a whole pack of these in one sitting.

Mid-Range Biscuits: perhaps best understood by what it is that lifts them above the entry-level biscuits. Primarily this is some form of seduction, such as some fruit, jam or maybe a revealing picture of the biscuit printed on thick glossy cellophane. Mid-range biscuits might even have their own strapline as footnote to their full-frontal picture, such as, 'I've got lovely crunchy oats', or 'Flat yet fruity'. Occasionally you'll find mid-range biscuits in corner shops and convenience stores: they are there to raise the tone. Beware of treating a mid-range biscuit with the same sort of off-hand disregard as entry-level biscuits: you may find yourself unwittingly eating the entire pack.

Luxury Biscuits: it would be a gross oversimplification to say luxury biscuits simply have chocolate on them and come in a box. However, that is their typical image. Most mid-range biscuits aspire to be luxury biscuits, and some think that simply by slapping on some chocolate and popping on a few extra wrappers everyone will be taken in. But it takes breeding to be a luxury biscuit, an established name in biscuit society and a really terrific box. Expect to see imperial or royal colours like purple and gold, and 'Since 1800 and something' written on the pack. Specifically look out for shortbread which has mad delusions of grandeur and often likes to pass itself off as 'luxury', despite simply being a bit of flour, sugar and butter. I don't know why it keeps on insisting that it's something special; it's embarrassing really.

Wifey says

Warning: Nicey went to university and did science stuff, which he likes, so you have to forgive him for going off on one every now and again. Now I failed A-level Maths, despite thinking I was very good at it. Because I can't be bothered remembering all that stuff, I've told those nice people at Time Warner to make all the science bits a different colour, so we non-science people (who really don't care about that sort of thing, and would need a lie down if we thought about it too much) can skip over it easily. Is that OK?

The Science Bit

One striking thing is how the shape of a biscuit-centric universe bears an uncanny resemblance to the Mandelbrot Set often referred to as the most complicated object in mathematics. Benoit Mandelbrot is a French mathematician whose work has led to a branch of mathematics called fractals, or fractal geometry. Mandelbrot Sets were hugely popular a few years ago as it used to take the average desktop computer all day to make the calculations needed to draw a picture of one. Now it takes only a few seconds, so their popularity has waned in favour of rudimentary animations of dancing kittens.

Fractal shapes like the Mandelbrot Set are often compared to forms of nature such as coastlines, tree bark and other gnarly stuff. It should not be left unsaid that some of the curly swirly bits around the edge of the Mandelbrot Set look just like the patterns on top of a Custard Cream. Of course, this could just be another coincidence, but they are starting to form a trend.

Venn Diagram

Even experienced biscuit eaters are sometimes bewildered about what exactly a biscuit is and what it isn't. They can easily be thrown into self-doubt by a simple Rusk or Flapjack. When does the combination of biscuit and chocolate cross from the realm of biscuits to the realm of confectionery? If there were easy answers to these questions people wouldn't be confused in the first place, and I wouldn't need to draw the Venn diagram of biscuits.

The Venn diagram was a very popular thing when I was at school. I remember for a week or two they were all the rage. The teacher would draw two large overlapping circles on the blackboard and then write our

47

names in them according to which of us had dogs, how many had cats, and who had dogs and cats. Of course, the kids with hamsters, rabbits and goldfish felt they had been glossed over, but that's life sometimes.

Venn diagrams were thought up by a chap called John Venn, who lived in the olden days. For the younger members of staff this is anything that predates *The Fimbles* and *Balamory*. He obviously enjoyed putting things into sets and thought that drawing circles around them was the way forward. He also had quite a large beard, and so probably predated the invention of the triple-blade razor.

Now a diagram like this is always going to raise more questions than it answers, so if you are expecting ultimate biscuit enlightenment be warned.

Biscuits form the centre, with crackers above and cake below. Running from left to right we move from bread into biscuits, then on to chocolate-covered biscuits until we reach confectionery in the shape of chocolate bars. The first thing to notice is that you can put very little store in the

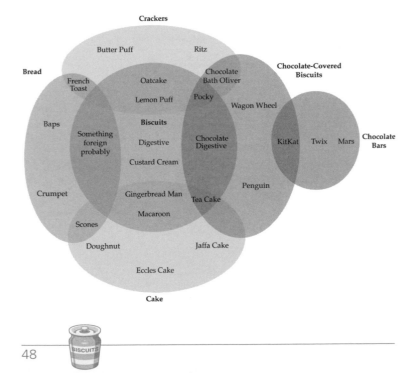

names of things. Just look at oatcakes. Clearly they are somewhere between biscuits and crackers, being an unsweetened oat biscuit, and so are not really a cake at all.

Gingerbread men cause more than their fair share of trouble, roaming across our Venn diagram. By no stretch of the imagination are they some form of bread, so they are swiftly moved along. They freely associate themselves with cakes, frequenting, as they are known to do, cake shops. It's no secret that underneath that icing and attached confectionery they are really a large man-shaped biscuit, so it's here in the union of cakes and biscuits that we'll allow them to go about their business. Occasionally at Easter or Christmas they are inclined to turn into rabbits or trees but they are not fooling anyone.

From Japan the exceedingly odd Pocky, a long straight pretzel 80 per cent dipped in chocolate, sits in the triple union of crackers, chocolate-covered biscuits and biscuits. That dark horse the KitKat sits in the union of chocolate bars and chocolate-covered biscuits, refusing to align itself with either side, enjoying as it does the best of both worlds.

The Jaffa Cake is drawn to the union of cake and chocolate-covered biscuits occupied by the Teacake. However, it must remain with its cake brethren by virtue of its sponge base. Meanwhile, the dreadful old Lemon Puff loiters close to its cousin next door in the crackers, the equally dubious Butter Puff.

Ideally the diagram should be drawn on the surface of a sphere, allowing crackers and cake to join, although I can't think what with. Rice cakes, possibly.

I'm sure by now that I've probably either confused or annoyed you. Either way, try drawing your own biscuit Venn diagram down the pub, over a cup of tea or maybe slipping it in to your next Powerpoint presentation if you are in the habit of making such things.

 # 8 Plain Dunkers

There is a lot of glamour in the biscuit world: enticing jam, seductive chocolate, tempting cream and abrasive sugar crusts. Alluring fruits such as the cranberry and guava are also adding exotic appeal to large soft-baked biscuit temptresses. It's all packaged in immodest boxes with cut-away cellophane panels or cartons with provocative and frilly lines. Oh yes, and they put the really good stuff on the top shelf in the supermarket, so that younger shoppers can't get their hands on them.

Then there are the plain old biscuits. A humble bunch, they are happy to be semi-submerged in a hot cuppa, their features swollen and barely legible, soaking up the scalding brew while we scarcely give them a second thought. Without them a great many cups of tea would be solitary affairs, devoid of biscuit companionship. They may not be glamorous, but they will still be around long after the appeal of the latest chocolate-clad bombshell or aspiring jam tart has ebbed away.

Rich Tea

Where would we be without the Rich Tea? It provides the ground floor on which the rest of the biscuit tower block rests. Without it we would be directionless. With it we have a marker that says, 'Above me it just gets better and better, while below are animal feeds, Spanish holiday biscuits and special medical biscuits from chemists'.'

The Rich Tea presents us straight away with a paradox. If these are 'Rich' Tea, where are 'Poor' Tea biscuits and what on earth do they taste like? Well, they would have to be fairly ropey old affairs because the Rich Tea itself is not exactly a self-contained one-biscuit flavour festival. We can only presume that 'Poor Tea' or even just 'Tea' was not the runaway success that Rich Tea has become.

What flavour it does manage to achieve comes from the various sugars in its recipe – sucrose, maltose and some glucose – plus a little bit of salt. So what are they good for? Dunking, of course. The Rich Tea can drive even the staunchest anti-dunker to dunk. It then comes into its own, convincing you that you have done the right thing by giving the eater the reward of sloppy, hot Rich Tea, which is actually better than what you started with.

So suitable for dunking is the Rich Tea that there are those who demand it as their biscuit of preference. Many builders, for example, seem to be chemically dependent on them, washed down with mugs of tea, two sugars please. If you are having substantial building work carried out it may be worth getting a case of Rich Tea in.

Most Rich Tea aficionados prefer the classic round Rich Tea, which is generally available in broad gauge and narrow gauge, depending on the brand. Whilst smaller-sized Rich Teas are easier to dunk than their larger brethren, many people seem to enjoy the challenge and skill needed to handle the big stuff. This explains the lesser popularity of the Rich Tea finger. However, those new to dunking will find the finger configuration much more predictable, being to dunking what rear-wheel stabilisers are to cycling. Nevertheless it should not be overlooked that the finger often seems to have the edge over its round sibling taste-wise, possibly due to its smaller build giving it a slightly higher bake.

There are attempts at turning the Rich Tea into something more enticing by covering them in chocolate or sticking some sort of cream up the middle, but it's all a bit akin to sticking a spoiler on the boot of your family car. There are a small band of people who seem to want a chunkier set version of the Rich Tea. Rather than be seen as purely aberrant they are occasionally catered for by some manufacturers, and therefore shouldn't cause a problem to the rest of us, other than harking on about it from time to time.

Marie

In the UK we have the Rich Tea. The rest of the world has the Marie. The Marie biscuit really isn't much to get worked up about. In fact, I'm struggling to think of anything to say about it. It's like a fluffy Rich Tea with a hint of vanilla. There. Oh, and it has some quite intricate patterns and writing. And some people use it as a vehicle for making a sandwich using soft butter. It is an essential part of the proceedings that little buttery worms can be extruded through the holes in the biscuit by pressing the two halves together.

India, Australia, South Africa and many other countries think of the Marie biscuit as part of their cuisine. How has this biscuit secured a position of global importance? No, that wasn't a rhetorical question: I really don't know. It must simply occupy the same ecological biscuit niche as the Rich Tea does in our biscuit environment. Just as in Australia where the large grassland grazers are not the northern hemisphere antelopes but kangaroos, so they have Marie biscuits rather than Rich Tea. The same goes for South Africa, but of course they actually do have antelopes. I think they are doing fine for deer in India, too.

Actually, I remember a splendid TV documentary about Indian wildlife where the stags of a type of wetland deer make a small scrape in the ground in which they urinate and then roll around in. After they are fairly well covered in that, they scrape up filthy bits of old moss and grass which they drape over their antlers. This apparently makes them irresistible to all the lady deer. I'm fairly sure I tried that in my student days too, but I don't recall it ever being successful.

Thin Arrowroot

Often found lurking among the other biscuits but never presenting more than one public-facing pack on the super-market shelves is the Thin Arrowroot. But why are they thin, and what on earth is Arrowroot? Well, the answer to the first lies in the second. Arrowroot is a starchy powder obtained from the rhizomes of the plant of the same name, grown in places like the West Indies. Typical uses for Arrowroot are to make a sort of gloopy fruit slop for desserts and the like, as it works a bit like corn flour. Adding arrowroot to biscuits seems to work a bit like adding sulphur to rubber to vulcanise it. Thin Arrowroots contain 2 per cent arrowroot and this appears to be enough to make them a bit like a really hard, dry and generally hostile Rich Tea.

I am more impressed with the structural properties of the biscuit than what it tastes like. For instance, the resonant frequencies possessed by the biscuit produced a higher note when dropped in comparison to a similar-sized Rich Tea. It therefore seems likely that such a thing as a 'Thick Arrowroot', while technically feasible, would be too much for the average consumer's dental facilities (although they would probably make terrific load-bearing walls). As result of this high level of structural integrity, the writing on top of the biscuits is fantastically detailed, as if engraved onto metal.

Older biscuit eaters remember when pubs used to have a jar of large Thin Arrowroots on the bar. Apparently these were given to children along with a glass of lemonade, or sometimes as a treat for dogs. Given that there was a war on, it would be unfair to suggest that these weren't genuine treats. However, it's easy to see why crisps, peanuts and Scampi fries caught on in the face of such competition.

There are also those who eat Thin Arrowroot biscuits as some sort of digestive aid, as its starch is easily digested. At only 2 per cent arrowroot you would have to eat an awful lot of biscuits before you gained much nutrition from that ingredient. The fresh mashed rhizomes of arrowroot are believed to be good for wounds from poisoned arrows, scorpion stings and spider bites. The biscuits, on the other hand, would probably be moderately deadly if you chucked them hard at spiders, scorpions and those aiming bows and arrows at you.

Morning Coffee

Back in the 1970s we used to watch a lot of *Kung Fu* on the telly. I was always impressed how he carried a small bag of dirt around with him, and used to add a pinch to a glass of water for a refreshing drink. As part of his training as a young apprentice monk, he had to walk down a long sheet of rice paper. His slow and presumably sweaty footsteps tore holes in the paper and he knew that he would be at monk school for some years to come. The answer may have been to substitute lino or a nice bit of carpet for rice paper, especially in high traffic areas like halls and kitchens. In fact, I would just stick to those flying-saucer sweets with sherbert inside as the predominant use for rice paper. No, the lesson was to go off and learn the whole 'being a monk' thing properly from the old fellow with the funny eyes.

As Wifey just said, 'What's this got to do with Morning Coffee?' Well, the Morning Coffee, like *Kung Fu*, first came to my attention during the 1970s. Having been raised in a household of keen biscuit eaters with progressive, liberal attitudes towards the baked snacks, it came as a shock that some people chose to eat such bland biscuits. In fact, I remember the first Morning Coffee I had while visiting my Aunty Sheila for 'morning coffee'. I was immediately struck by its intricate graphics. The Morning Coffee held out the promise of sophistication, of hidden depths in order to fulfil its stated mission as a pre-lunch coffee biscuit. Unlike *Kung Fu*, the Morning Coffee didn't have an associated hit record ('Everybody Was Morning Coffee Eating'), however, I was still keen to taste this 'now' biscuit. It was a bitter blow to find that essentially it was a turncoat Rich Tea. Those intricate pictures of coffee pots and wisps of steam were the only noteworthy point to the biscuit. The rewards to be had from nibbling out the coffee pot from the biscuit compared to, say, a 'cow-ectomy' performed on a Malted Milk were scant. A simple mental note to avoid the Morning Coffee for the rest of my life appeared to be the answer.

Now, some thirty years later, fate has conspired to confront me with that knobbly rectangle of biscuit under-achievement once again. The local branch of the Macmillan Cancer Relief charity run an annual event called 'The World's Biggest Coffee Morning' and they got in touch to see which biscuit I would recommend for such an

occasion. I explained to the nice Canadian organising lady on the phone, 'You'll need some Morning Coffees then.' 'Good and what cookies do you recommend?' she replied, never having heard of the Morning Coffee biscuit and assuming I was being evasive and odd. 'Who makes them?' she continued. I admitted I had no idea, as I couldn't think of a branded Morning Coffee, but replied that all the big supermarkets have them.

I thought I had better get some in case I had to answer any tricky questions. So here I am staring into a biscuit tin of Morning Coffees, reaping what I have sown. Well, I couldn't recommend them and not try them again. We grabbed a pack from two different supermarkets: the biscuits appear to be identical; no doubt they are. I'm sure past Morning Coffees had pictures of coffee pots on them but these have resorted to a simple cup and saucer image. Maybe it's because the coffee pot itself has been relegated to such niches as the hotel breakfast, and certainly isn't used regularly in the domestic setting.

A little while ago I backed myself into a corner, resulting in my taste testing seven types of Rich Tea side by side. Some may have been scarred for life with the memory of such a trial. In fact, some raw recruits to Nicey's biscuit-tasting boot camp were. However, I vowed to become a better biscuit reviewer through the experience. And now finally we get to the point: *the Morning Coffee, when compared to most types of Rich Tea, is ever so slightly tastier!* I was, of course, shocked to my very core, my whole belief system threatening to crumble before me. How could this be? Well, ingredient number four is malt extract. This, it seems, has given the Morning Coffee a very faint malty sweetness, earning a small measure of individuality other than its pictures of cups and steam.

His Rich Tea lesson learnt, Nicey notes the slight difference in taste and skips over the tricky rice paper of bland biscuit sampling leaving not a single footmark.

 Shortcake

It's very difficult to pin down what is exactly meant by shortcake. The 'short' part refers to the fat in the recipe that has the effect of making the baked biscuit soft and crumbly. One explanation offered is that the fat serves to 'shorten' the gluten molecules from the wheat, which makes for a less rigid molecular structure. The biscuits in this section either completely or loosely fall into the shortcake biscuit category. Of course, you may aggressively disagree with my choices, in which case you might want to consider some sort of anger-management counselling. After all, we are only trying to sort out a few biscuits.

Shorties

Ah, the simple shortcake biscuit or 'Shortie': always there to bulk out the biscuit tin or make up the numbers in a family biscuit assortment. A steady performer, the Shortie is often overlooked but is always a welcome sight on

the biscuit plate. It comes into its own in those little packs of biscuits you get in hotel rooms, which the biscuit eater will greet like a long-lost friend.

However, the shortcake has a surprising history which we can trace back to the pagan winter solstice festivals. In Scotland, large round oatcake Bannocks were baked with the edges decorated with sun rays, as people looked forward to the return of the summer sun. At Hogmanay the 'First Footers' (the first to set foot in the house after midnight) would be required to bring with them a bottle of whisky and a Bannock at the very least. Providing they were dark haired (a good sign of not being a Viking), and not a minister, doctor or gravedigger, then they could expect a kiss from the ladies of the house. The intermingling of Christian and pagan elements sees us buying Yuletide tins of Scottish shortbread complete with their sun-ray design to give away as Christmas presents.

Traditionally, any small, round shortcake biscuit will emulate its ancestors with the sun's rays scalloping around its rim, and a pattern of marks on its centre. As we move to the workaday rectangular Shortie, the edge pattern and prick marks are retained, telling us that this is a mini-shortbread. Perhaps small self-contained 'First Footer' kits could be made using a three-pack of shortbread fingers and a whisky miniature.

Lincoln

Technically, the Lincoln is a short-dough biscuit, and belongs to the larger family of shortcake biscuits. It's a very serviceable biscuit, not so nice that you would want to eat a truckload, but not so bland that you can't cheerfully tuck several away in a session.

What is really exciting about the Lincoln is the pattern of dots on the top.

Now it appears that the pattern of dots can take two forms: concentric circles as shown on the McVitie's one here, or a tightly packed pattern a bit like that formed by the ends of pipes which have been stacked up. So what are the dots for? I like to think that they give the Lincoln superior traction, affording the eater a great non-slip grip. As is their custom, McVitie's have also tried to emboss the word 'Lincoln' on to the biscuit, which shouldn't be necessary, given the distinctive dots.

Our good friend and fellow biscuit enthusiast Mandy often recounts the tale of her mother's experimental Lincoln biscuit trifle. I'm assured by Mandy that anybody contemplating pushing the envelope of trifle technology in a similar direction really shouldn't bother.

Abernethy (vs Bath Oliver)

I have to admit to being a very recent convert to the Abernethy biscuit. The best-known examples are made in Edinburgh by Simmers and have a distinctive red and yellow pack; so much so that I was possibly slightly and fairly irrationally intimidated by them. When I finally did pluck up the courage to buy a pack, it was all very easy. The anticipated probing look from the checkout girl never happened. And the biscuit itself? Well, they are very nice actually, a bit like a cross between an All Butter and a shortcake. The biscuit mix is raised with ammonium bicarbonate. Apparently this means they smell a bit odd prior to baking.

Abernethy biscuits are named after their Scottish inventor, Dr John Abernethy, who in turn was probably named after the Scottish town. The town takes its name from the Gaelic word 'aber', which doesn't mean platform-heeled Viking singing group but 'mouth of', and 'Nethy' which is the name of a river. In the past biscuit inventing seems to have been a very popular activity for doctors, and it's a shame that they don't do it today. Information like 'Dr D. Taylor MB, BS, MRCGP with a special interest in orthopaedics and making a new sort of jam ring' would be of use when registering with a medical practice.

The other famous biscuit-inventing doctor was Dr William Oliver, who invented the Bath Oliver in the mid-eighteenth century. The Bath Oliver is a cracker gravitating naturally towards the cheese board, but its rare chocolate-covered version is best described as a biscuit. Bath Olivers are so named because Dr Oliver invented them in Bath, while serving as the physician to those visiting the famous spa for its restorative waters. Just as eating salted nuts or crisps is going to have you gasping for a drink, drinking pints of Bath water would probably have you craving something dry and moistureless. Not only was Dr Oliver's cracker suitably non-wet, it contained a very small amount of hops, which were presumably in there for their active properties. Just to make sure everybody knew who invented them, Bath Olivers are stamped with a picture of the late Dr Oliver and the words 'Dr Oliver Inventor'.

It is said that upon his death, Dr Oliver bequeathed the recipe to his coachman, Atkins, along with four bags of flour and a sizeable amount of cash. Most people would have retired to the country with the cash to live on pancakes, but Atkins chose to open a shop selling the crackers and became a rich man. Apparently the shop is now a pub in Green Street, not far from the Roman Baths. Huntley & Palmer's took over baking of the Bath Oliver and today they are made by Jacob's under licence from Fortts, who acquired the recipe in the 1950s.

We'll never know who would have won a head-to-head biscuit inventing competition between Dr Abernethy and Dr Oliver. I think Dr Oliver certainly appears to be the madder of the two, and as such would have been a fairly unpredictable adversary. Dr Abernethy, on the other hand, would be drawing on an extensive cultural background of Scottish biscuit making and so would probably come up with much more sensible and plausible designs. So my money would be on him.

All About Hydrogenated Fat

Fat molecules have long chains of carbon atoms with a couple of hydrogen atoms to each one of carbon. Oils from plants tend to have a double bond in the chain between two of the carbons and can only join to one hydrogen. These are called **unsaturated fats** as not all the carbons are saturated with hydrogen atoms. Now, one double bond in the chain and you have a monosaturate. More than one double bond and you have a **polyunsaturated fat**. Hoorah for organic chemistry and margarine. Unsaturated fats have a lower melting point than the saturated fats from animals, which is why the fat from plants forms liquid oils, and that from animals forms solids like butter and lard. Eating a diet that has unsaturated fat is considered to be healthy, and it also provides so-called essential 'fatty acids', which are ones our bodies can't make for themselves.

Hydrogenation, by contrast, is an industrial process which stuffs extra hydrogen into the molecules, removing the double bonds as it does so. The resulting **hydrogenated vegetable fat** will tend to be a solid at room temperature rather than a liquid. This is basically the way in which margarine is made. Yes, I know, nothing funny here yet.

Partial hydrogenation doesn't quite finish the job and produces some fairly exotic compounds called **trans-fats** that wouldn't normally occur in our diet. Current advice from the UK Food Standards Agency and the US FDA associates trans-fats with raised blood cholesterol levels, via a lowering of LDL and a raising of HDL cholesterol. Yes, nothing funny here either, but now you know.

So, like many things in modern life, there are upsides and downsides to all of this, and the old adage 'all things in moderation' coupled with a well-balanced diet and regular exercise seems to be the advice from all quarters.

All Butter

The first thing that you notice about an All Butter biscuit is that it's not all butter. If it were, it would indeed be butter, and therefore be suitable for spreading on toast. Judging from the lack of warnings to this effect on the packet, it appears that people don't routinely make this mistake.

The All Butter biscuit gets its name from the fact that its fat content is derived from butter alone. That's got to be good: butter is fine, wholesome stuff. Typically biscuits use something called hydrogenated vegetable oil, which has physical characteristics that make it suited to biscuit manufacture: it produces biscuits with the desired sort of texture; it's also cheaper than butter and produces a biscuit with a longer shelf life, which helps keep the cost to consumers low.

If you are concerned about hydrogenated fats stick to All Butter biscuits: they cost a bit more but they do taste superb. One can easily imagine that these were baked specially for you by your aunty or some skilled biscuit-making acquaintance.

Malted Milk

I get so carried away talking about this utterly fantastic biscuit that sometimes I sense people becoming slightly tense and uneasy, as if concerned for their personal safety. Still, it is easy to get overexcited about a biscuit that has dairy cattle embossed on to it. Known to many simply as 'Cow biscuits', they have perhaps the finest artwork of any biscuit ever.

Malted Milks are the Elgin Marbles of the biscuit world, except without any of the accompanying controversy. Just look at the picture: it's got a standing-up cow and another one sitting down. The second cow is the cause of some confusion among biscuit eaters, often being mistaken for a calf due to its smaller size. In fact, it's another heifer placed further away in the scene: that's perspective, a drawing technique refined by Renaissance artists. The first cow grazes and the second ruminates while sitting down, no doubt relaxing after some hectic grazing. The skilled 'Cow biscuit' eater will be able to nibble off the outer bits of the biscuit to leave just the cows, which surely are the most delicious bits. If I were some kind of sultan bloke I would no doubt have my harem busily nibbling the cows out of Malted Milks for me.

One thing that does trouble me about this aspect of the Malted Milk is that there are no mirror-image Malted Milks. If such things existed then it would be possible to place two nibbled-out cows back-to-back to create a whole three-dimensional biscuit cow. This would be an event much like an alignment of the planets, or the deciphering of the Rosetta Stone. If they were the excellent half chocolate-coated sub-species then no doubt both halves could be coaxed to adhere to each other with some gentle melting of the chocolate. It's hard to face the bitter truth that we will never see this.

If all of that weren't enough excitement for one biscuit, there's also the fact that they taste fantastic due to the malt used in their recipe. It's the interplay between this and the intense sweetness of sucrose that gives the Malted Milk its wonderful and rich flavour.

How Malt is Made

Malt is made by allowing barley grains to begin to germinate, spraying them with warm water and gently turning them. Enzymes in the seed begin the work of converting the stored starch into useful sugar that can be used by the growing seed. An enzyme called maltase breaks down the long chains of glucose molecules that form the starch into the simple disaccharide of two joined glucose molecules, malt-ose. At this point the whole lot is brought abruptly to a halt by a good swift roasting, the length of which determines if any of the sugars caramelise to give an even more complex sweetness. A bit more processing and the sticky foodstuff malt is produced, which can be used as the raw ingredient of beer or, just as nobly, find itself in the biscuit factory.

Sports Biscuit

There was a point when I thought the Sports biscuit had gone to the big biscuit tin in the sky. Another shortcake biscuit, its recipe seems to have drifted from Malted Milk to Lincoln over the years. Its real claim on biscuit fame is the relief pictures of stickmen playing various sports.

Back in the 1970s they used to confine their sporting activities mainly to proper Olympic sports, and a smattering of football and tennis. Even with their fairly limited sporting prowess not all of the sports were easy to spot, with the water-based ones being particularly tricky. Water polo was probably the hardest sport to recognise from all the little lines and circles. Given their stick-like design, there wasn't much scope for nibbling out the figures, so once the sport was identified the biscuit could be munched down without ceremony.

After a quest a couple of years ago to find the Sports biscuit, it turned up safe and sound in a Welsh Kwik Save. After a bit more searching we found that Fox's Biscuits, who make a great deal of the biscuits for Marks and Spencer, now supply the Sports biscuit to most major supermarkets. Today stickmen can be seen skateboarding, but the basic intention remain the same: a cheerful little shortcake-style biscuit.

Trying to get a handle on the vast quantities of biscuits produced by factories is obviously fraught with drawbacks which is why we have developed the standard measurement of 'How long to reach the moon'. This is the amount of biscuit production measured in years, months and days to reach the moon when the biscuits are laid end to end. Ideally we would have thought up a really snappy name for this unit of measurement, like the light year or the parsec, but we haven't. Perhaps this is something you could worry about on our behalf, maybe on your way to work or while waiting in a long queue of traffic.

If we were to use Tunnock's Wafers, it would take nineteen years and ten months to reach the moon. As for interstellar travel, it would take 514 million years to make enough of them to stretch for one light year. If we go back in time 514 million years that puts us in the late Cambrian period at the start of the Palaeozoic era: at this time most creatures looked like the sort of creepy-crawly stuff that lives in your compost heap, only bigger, and fish hadn't even been invented.

Switching to the Penguin as a means of space travel, we find that we can get to the moon and back twice in one year. That's enough to build a sort of square tube thing, which would no doubt be especially handy in space. As for interstellar travel, the Penguin is going to take about 6.5 million years to travel a light year, which is fairly brisk. That's about how long it took for mankind to evolve from those proto-human guys who looked like nightclub bouncers.

 # Digestives

The undisputed king of the large-diameter biscuits, this is truly an iconic biscuit. It was originally conceived as an aid to digestion, due to the amount of baking soda (sodium bicarbonate) used in its recipe. This explanation seems a little contrived to me: the baking soda would decompose under the heat of baking to release carbon dioxide, thereby raising the biscuit and making itself ineffectual as a digestive aid, other than via its accompanying payload of roughage.

Unfortunately, poor-quality Digestives tend to taste like damp cardboard, and can easily pull the whole genre into disrepute. On the other hand, a good one is a thing of wonder and sustenance. As I found out on a walking holiday in Wales many years ago, sheep seem to feel the same way about Digestives. While sat atop a lonely Welsh peak in the mist and drizzling rain, brewing a cuppa on my camping stove and munching on Digestives, ovine faces began appearing in the gloom. Eventually we were surrounded by a small flock who quickly breached our defences and made off with five or six biscuits before we managed to regroup and fend them off by quickly improvising gruff sheep-scaring noises.

The Digestive

Found in two main varieties, sweetmeal and wholemeal, the Digestive sets a standard for the whole biscuit world. Its satisfying nature and large size make the biscuit eater pause to consider how many to take at a time: one, two or maybe three. As biscuits go, the Digestive has quite a lot of salt in it, which can lead it into trouble with cheese and other acquaintances. The unwary Digestive can often be found covered in strange toppings, which

I always think is demeaning to its nature. It's a bit like when rugby players appear in drag, or elderly dogs are forced to wear hats, sunglasses and dresses by little girls because they are too lethargic to make a run for it. Having said that, there is one Digestive that positively seeks out this sort of attention, and that's the one shaped like a little loaf of Hovis bread. It happily associates itself with all sorts of undesirable characters such as the Butter Puff and the High Baked Water Biscuit to form a selection of crackers and biscuits for cheese. It's not uncommon to see it tottering around with a slice of Edam and mandarin orange segment stuck on top of it. Mind you, it does tend to do this at Christmas and it's easy to go a little off the rails and make a spectacle of oneself at Yuletide.

The Digestive is no stranger to the ways of dunking and would bid against many other old-school biscuits, such as the Rich Tea or Gingernut, to claim the crown of archetypal dunker. However, its large diameter can create awkward social situations when paired with a mug or cup of a smaller diameter. Dunk, nibble, rotate is the usual way out of this dilemma. That said, it's quite common for the Digestive to break obligingly in two. This fills the biscuit eater with mixed emotions as they come to terms with the disintegration of their previously pristine Digestive. The upside is they now can quickly and humanely dispatch the little fella in three or four swift dunks.

As a young man at university I often saw girls slip a sheet of kitchen roll in the bottom of their biscuit tins when opening a new packet of Digestives. I imagine this was to catch the crumbs. Although completely unnecessary, I always found it somewhat alluring. I was used to eating them straight from the pack, which also did a good job of catching the crumbs (they could then be polished off in much the same way as the bits at the bottom of crisp bags). I'm not aware if this more direct approach to crumb containment was ever considered to be alluring by girls. I've probably just answered my own question there.

Milk Chocolate Digestive

There can be few biscuits which garner such respect as the McVitie's Chocolate Digestive. Referred to by most as simply 'chocolate biscuits', they provide a figurehead for the entire chocolate biscuit world. They were created in 1925 by McVitie's in Edinburgh, and are made today at Europe's biggest biscuit factory in Harlesden in London, which produces 4,860,000 or thereabouts of them every day.

Due in no small part to the quality of its chocolate-less brother the Digestive, upon which it is based, McVitie's simply outclass all other contenders. Mind you, they did invent the Digestive, or rather an ambitious young Scottish baker called Alexander Grant did. He came up with it about five years after beginning work for Robert McVitie in Edinburgh at the end of the nineteenth century. Some thirty years later and they popped some milk chocolate on top to create this classic.

The distinctive horizontal and vertical patterning in the chocolate serves to distinguish the McVitie's instantly from other, lesser biscuits. The quantity of chocolate used shows thoughtful restraint, resulting in a harmonious balance of biscuit and topping. This is good to see in these times when an almost vulgar overuse of chocolate seems to be the norm. We sometimes seem to be in danger of drowning in a sea of mediocre chocolate excess, at the expense of the biscuit buried below. The Chocolate Digestive shows us that 29 per cent milk chocolate brings just enough sweet indulgence to tell our taste buds that we are being spoilt, while still allowing the satisfying biscuit taste plenty of space.

People of my generation carry round with them a chocolate biscuit-related trauma thanks to the legendary 1970s British animated series, *Bagpuss*. Bagpuss was a saggy old cloth cat, who belonged to Emily. Due to special magic, he would awaken and as he came to life so too would the other toys and objects around him, such as Professor Yaffle, the carved wooden woodpecker bookend, and the carved mice on the front of the mouse organ. Part of the brilliance of any of the works of Oliver Postgate and Peter Firmin, the show's creators, was the emotional range in their little films, which made all their characters and the worlds they inhabited completely real. It was this which contributed to my issue with chocolate biscuits.

In the episode 'The Mouse Mill' Emily produces a box containing the Marvellous Mechanical Mouse Mill. The mice open it up and begin using it as a biscuit factory, manufacturing chocolate biscuits from breadcrumbs and butter beans. As a ten-year-old I quite happily accepted this, although I remember wondering where they were getting the chocolate from. However, magic was often at work in the world of Bagpuss, so I made allowances and was happy to accept that this was a possible means by which chocolate biscuits could be made. I still remember clearly the bitter disappointment when Professor Yaffle revealed that the mice simply had one ready-made chocolate biscuit which they kept producing from round the back. If nothing else, I learnt never to take a reanimated carved wooden mouse at its word, and always to look behind Mechanical Mouse Mills, marvellous or not. To this day I check the ingredients on the back of a packet of Chocolate Digestives from time to time to see if butter beans are in there. If they ever do turn up, I won't be in the least bit surprised.

Apparently McVitie's arrive at the output figure of fifty-two biscuits a second by dividing down the annual metric tonnage of biscuits baked. Right now McVitie's estimate that they produce some seventy-one million packs of Chocolate Digestives a year, which surely is a big number. However, a while back, an amusing slip, which was promptly corrected, on their website had managed to change the word 'year' for 'day'. This had us eating sixty-five million packs a day, which I calculated as 1.12 packs for every man, woman and child in the country. Put another way, it meant that the Nice Cup Of Tea And A Sit Down weekly provisions should include thirty-one packs of chocolate digestives. Some of our plucky correspondents suggested ways of accounting for the 23.6 billion extra packets of Chocolate Digestives McVitie's should really be selling each year. One chap helpfully suggested that cash and carries do buy a 'hell of a lot of biscuits all at once'.

Dark Chocolate Digestive

Something that has always impressed me is the fierce loyalty shown by those who prefer the dark chocolate variant of the Chocolate Digestive. Despite being in the minority, they behave in a somewhat superior way, believing that only they, the elite, can appreciate the true chocolate biscuit, a dark chocolate biscuit. The usual implication is that dark chocolate is for the grown-ups. This dark chocolate superiority complex is not confined to the Digestive and extends to other chocolate biscuits.

If that were as far as it went that would be fine. However, all too often the dark chocolate faction can't help but pass off their opinions as facts. Where a harmless 'I prefer the dark chocolate ones' would suffice, they have to push it with provocative statements such as 'The dark chocolate ones are best'. This is tantamount to spoiling for a fight. However, most people will let it go, as the votes have been counted and the dark chocolate guys lost so it's not worth coming to blows.

If you've ever tried constructing any sort of large building out of biscuits then you'll know that it has its fair share of drawbacks. That's not to say it can't be done, but you may have to cheat a bit and maybe mix up a biscuit cement by crushing some up and adding melted butter or margarine. Then simply pop the whole lot into your fridge for about thirty minutes and your new property will be ready to use. Of course, you're going to need a huge fridge for this, so a handy tip is to make prefabricated sections that just about fit. These can simply be slotted together and fastened using some extra jam, butter, chocolate spread, peanut butter or something.

Your biscuit house is obviously going to attract enormous numbers of ants, wasps, maggots and rats, which is going to be embarrassing as you show friends and family around. This could also be offputting to a potential buyer, should you wish to sell. Your estate agent, who is earning a month's salary for approximately two hours' work, may suggest that you describe this as 'rustic charm' or a 'haven for wildlife'. I would expect starlings are going to find it very easy to nest in your roof as well. Let's face it, starlings can get into anything – wood, slate, UPVC soffits and facia boards – so chocolate biscuits are going to be no problem.

Should you happen to be the witch out of Hansel and Gretel, then you'll know that children can be a particular source of problems to a biscuit dwelling. Apparently boys are likely to eat your roof, while girls will munch their way through your clear sugar windows. You can lessen the risk to your residence by choosing a site that's well away from places frequented by the under twelves. A clearing in the deepest, darkest part of the forest is a very popular choice for many witches. This is obviously going to make access to your property less than straightforward, and services such as mains sewerage are probably not going to be available. Still, if you plan on commuting by broomstick and you don't mind having a septic tank then this shouldn't present a problem.

It's almost inevitable that from time to time a couple of little lost children are somehow going to make it through to your isolated clearing. Typically they'll be leaving a trail of breadcrumbs behind themselves as a means of retracing their steps and subsequently finding their way back home. Unfortunately for you and for them the local birds seem to have acquired a taste for baked offerings. Any that are still capable of flight after gorging themselves on your roofing will simply swoop down and polish off the breadcrumb trail as well. After they have polished them off they'll be back over to your gaff to see off your skirting boards.

As a witch, you'll be wanting to roast or boil any children that come your way. Obviously in this day and age that just simply isn't acceptable. So why not try microwaving them on full power for no more than twenty minutes: this will leave your evening free for coven meetings and the like.

Wifey says

Oh dear. Time for Nicey to take a holiday, I think.

Hansel and Gretel ■

Chocolate Caramel

The chocolate and Digestive innovation has continued apace and a mere seventy years after the introduction of the original Chocolate Digestive along came the Chocolate Caramel from McVitie's. This is basically like a narrow-gauge Chocolate Digestive, with a layer of caramel slipped in between the biscuit and the chocolate. It takes even the prepared eater a little by surprise as the biscuit has a little more fight in it than your average chocolate biscuit, ensuring that you don't eat them all in one go. The caramel acts almost like a layer of tasty glue. If they weren't so tasty, I would constantly be put in mind of vinyl floor tiles stuck to MDF with lashings of brown tile adhesive. However, that image very rarely comes to mind, unless I think about it, as I'm doing now.

# Gingernuts

There are few biscuits I can think of that are so emphatically of their genre and yet vary so much from manufacturer to manufacturer as the Gingernut. Perhaps the closest analogy lies in the world of single-malt whiskeys (yes, that's right, I meant to put the 'e' in denoting Irish whiskey as that's Wifey's favourite tipple). Whiskey is all made from the same stuff: water, malted barley and yeast. This is fermented, distilled and put into oak casks. After some years it's bottled, we buy it and Wifey drinks it with an ice-cube. Simple. Well, evidently not given all the different brands and prices that there are to choose from (and to be perfectly fair the different flavours and tastes). As with whiskey, so with the Gingernut: from a few simple ingredients comes a surprising and delightful variety.

The Gingernut is the spiciest biscuit in the tin and can range from a rich warm mellowness to a fiery tongue tingler. All Gingernuts should be crisp and crunchy; if they are not then they are either stale or not Gingernuts. It is thought the 'nut' in the name comes purely from their physicality and from the Middle English 'nute' or Olde English 'hnutu', which used to be the appellation for all sorts of small, hard things. So Gingernut conveys not only the flavour but also the texture.

Actually, talking of Olde English, it has always puzzled me that the refreshment trolley on the 8.15 to King's Cross always has two cans of cider on it. Who exactly starts the day with two cans of cider? Well, so far nobody, as they are inexorably there. This reminds me of the sign in the window of the lounge bar of the Britannia Inn in Pencoed, South Wales, which from about 1972 until 1981 said, 'Always something hot to eat'. The sign was a daily feature of village life to anybody who had ever waited outside the 'Brit' for the level-crossing gates on the main London to Swansea line to open. We would often wonder exactly what the hot edible thing could be. My friend Clust, a budding Welsh hippy, asked the landlord, Dilwyn, what exactly it was they had hot to eat. He replied, 'Well, we've got a pasty.' Clust took up the offer of the pasty, anointed it with brown sauce and pepper, and washed it down with two pints of Welsh bitter. A few days later the sign was permanently removed.

Similarly, I'm often tempted to buy the two cans of cider on the 8.15 to King's Cross to see if they ever return. Maybe, like the mystery of the pasty, the world would be forever altered from that point on. I look at the other passengers, trying to work out if any of them have noticed that the two cans of cider in the bottom of the trolley could be a potential cusp for humanity. If we cross that threshold we might enter a new age of cider-less early morning commuter trains.

So why are Gingernuts capable of such diversity? From where I'm sitting, it's down to two things: sugar and ginger. The sugar, depending on the recipe, may be refined white sugar or less refined brown and demerara sugars. It is also present as golden syrup, molasses or black treacle, all of which have their own balance of component sugars: sucrose, glucose and fructose. The ginger, meanwhile, is usually added in the form of ground ginger, which is the dried and powdered rhizome of the ginger plant *Zingiber officinale*. The roots are scraped of their smooth outer skin, dried in the sun and then ground to produce powdered ginger. The best ginger in the world comes from Jamaica, and when combined with Caribbean sugar from sugar cane it seems that the Gingernut is really a West Indian treat.

With any biscuit the baking is crucial to its final taste and appearance, and never more so than the Gingernut: the deep brown colour is caused by the caramelising of the sugar to form a sweet brittle toffee which gets puffed up by the raising agent. Gingernuts start life as little flattened balls of mix and the heat of the oven makes the mix runny so it sinks down and flattens out. It also causes bubbles of carbon dioxide to be produced from the raising agent which puffs up the biscuit, filling it with little air pockets. The interplay of these three processes leads to such subtleties as where the cracks are formed on the surface, how brittle the biscuit is, and – crucially – how much tea it soaks up.

Anybody who has munched Gingernuts while looking at a computer monitor across a room may have noticed odd visual disturbances which occur as the illusion of persistence of vision is interrupted by the clatter inside your mouth. Momentary black flashes appear on the monitor. In these days of LCD monitors and high refresh rates it's becoming a rarer phenomenon, but it's still worth trying out if you can.

Oh dear. I'm giving myself quite an unnatural Gingernut craving writing this, which isn't going to be made better as we take a look at some wonderful examples of the genre.

Types of Gingernut

Perhaps the most famous Gingernut in the UK is made by McVitie's. A very dark biscuit that uses molasses in its recipe, it has a little calm zone in the middle of the biscuit where the cracks and fissures don't venture. McVitie's have also added a little lemon oil which provides a subtle zesty note against the rich warm sweetness. Overall, the McVitie's has a rich sweetness with spicy fragrant notes from the ginger. If it were a whiskey then it would be a blend of spirits aged in sherry and rum casks, I expect.

On the other side of the planet, from New Zealand, comes the Griffin's Gingernut. It has a wonderful elegance and simplicity, which allows its ginger flavour to burst out with a peppery exuberance. The cracks on its

surface have a homogeneous distribution, and its recipe uses brown sugar. But the really impressive thing about the Griffin's Gingernut is how hard it is. While the McVitie's offers a nice hard biscuit which soon yields to give a pleasant munchy mouthful, the Griffin's presents much more of a challenge. In fact, if these were indeed nuts I would rate the McVitie's as a pecan with the Griffin's as a Brazil and a control Digestive as, say, a peanut shell. To use our whiskey analogy, I would have to say that the Griffin's is a fine single malt aged in bourbon casks (the spirit not the biscuit).

Another UK favourite is the Marks and Spencer Gingernut, which has a lovely golden colour and a light, open texture. Again there is a good distribution of cracks on its surface. A syrupy sweetness with bright but restrained ginger notes makes this a very vulnerable biscuit pack, which can easily sustain heavy losses from even the most casual biscuit eater. As a whiskey I would see it as one of those broadly appealing blends that slips down without a second thought.

As if to justify my stance on the Gingernut, the Australian biscuit-making legend Arnott's produce four different types using Queensland ginger. At one time Arnott's had four bakeries serving the various states, each baking its Gingernuts in its own way. In Queensland Gingernuts are thin and sweet, with a dark colour. In New South Wales they are small, thick and hard, with a light colour. In Victoria and Tasmania they are bigger, softer and sweeter. And in South and Western Australia, the biscuits look similar to their Victorian cousins, but taste sweeter. When Arnott's experimented with a unified pan-Australian Gingernut, their taste tests told them that people preferred their own local variety. So to this day Arnott's still produce four regional variations. Go on, it's your turn to think of a whiskey analogy.

 Oats

Oats have long been a valuable source of sustenance for both mankind and the Scottish. For generations the humble oatcake has been made from oats and water baked on a hot stone. While no doubt nutritious and full of slow-release carbohydrate and dietary fibre, they still make a Rich Tea seem like an extravagantly sweet and fanciful treat. Then along came oats' soulmate, golden syrup, in 1881, courtesy of Lyles. Oats and golden syrup complement each other superbly well, and are the basis for Flapjacks, Anzac biscuits and the biscuits in this section. From time to time you'll see golden syrup listed in ingredients as 'partially invert refiner's sugar', but it's just being coy.

Lyles' distinctive and odd logo is a dead lion with bees swarming around it, apparently choosing to make a nest inside the carcass. Underneath is written, 'Out of the strong came forth sweetness'. We have Samson of the long hair and temple-knocking-down fame to thank for that line. As an adult, Nanny Nicey was very disappointed to find out that her firmly held childhood belief that dead lions are an integral part of the production of golden syrup wasn't so. If bees really were routinely keen on using dead animals as nesting sites then Winnie the Pooh might have been a much more macabre book.

Abbey Crunch

The 'original oat biscuit' was how the sadly missed Abbey Crunch described itself. The last production run was made in September 2003, and closed the book on what was for me an inspirational biscuit. When I started my website, the very first biscuit I chose to review was the Abbey Crunch.

I remember my first encounter with it in the 1970s in my nan's house in Essex, which is where the Abbey Crunch claims its heritage (Essex, not my nan's house). In the 1970s most biscuits were in clear cellophane wrap with some overprinting. The dark blue packaging with the golden biscuit standing out vividly was like nothing else I had ever seen.

Perhaps it was the name that let my nan feel comfortable experimenting with such dazzling packaging. Apparently based on a recipe used by the monks of the Abbey of St John the Baptist, Colchester, the Abbey Crunch was baked by McVitie's, who put a picture of the abbey on the packs. A more convincing bloodline is given via the prewar Colchester baker Priory Biscuits, who produced a crunchy oat biscuit based on a recipe given to its owner Frank Curtis by his mother. I'm inclined to believe this, as the main ingredient in an Abbey Crunch is sugar, something which would have been unknown to eleventh-century monks.

There has always been an affinity between oats and sugar, which is played out in many biscuits and cakes. The pairing evokes images of wholesome homemade biscuits and Flapjacks with nutty savoury notes. I was thus astounded by the brittle toffee sweetness of the Abbey Crunch when my nan first produced them. I think she quickly realised that the packs of Petit Beurre biscuits that she used to buy in the Hadleigh branch of Safeway would no longer be an option. Actually, the Petit Beurre were never really an option, and I started to suspect my biscuit leanings came from my paternal lineage. (Although I have yet to display my dad's liking for eating a big stack of High Baked Water Biscuits, or three or four Cream Crackers unaccompanied by any form or topping or spread. Mind you, a cup of tea was usually required fairly soon after.)

I personally believe that without the Abbey Crunch we could never have had its descendant, the wildly popular HobNob. Indeed, as McVitie's try to console those who miss the Abbey Crunch, they often point them towards the HobNob.

HobNob

McVitie's rolled out the HobNob in the mid-1980s, capturing the biscuit-buying public's attention with this oat biscuit and creating an overnight classic. The HobNob was simply a *tour de force*, ticking all the boxes for a successful new biscuit. Most important was the taste, and by turning to the oat once again McVitie's were able to achieve that tasty and slightly irregular charm. The oaty knobbles made the HobNob seem less manufactured than its contemporaries and no doubt contributed to its name. A relatively large diameter and suitable thickness made it both satisfying and a great dunker.

The HobNob achieved one of those rare feats for new products by being simultaneously new and yet familiar, as if we were merely being reintroduced after an unexplained absence. Could this have been an echo of the Abbey Crunch in the biscuit-eating public's mind, or was it simply the disarming and approachable oat at work? The cheerful orange pack, the strap line 'One nibble and you're nobbled' and, of course, the name all helped to place the biscuit comfortably on the stage of UK biscuits. The name begged not to be taken seriously, and told us that this was a biscuit for the honest masses, at the time of the rise of the yuppie in Britain under Margaret Thatcher.

After two years the HobNob was firmly cemented into the biscuit landscape of the nation and ready to don its ennobling covering of milk chocolate. This was closely followed by a plain chocolate variety. I can remember exactly where I was standing when I first heard of the plain chocolate version, much in the way people remember where they were when they heard of the assassination of Kennedy. Obviously, it wasn't quite that dramatic; it just oddly located itself near the front of my mind rather than at the back. What's even stranger is that the plain chocolate ones are my least favourite.

The Chocolate HobNob is also a fairly sure bet when looking for a romantic biscuit with which to woo the opposite sex. I have had couples tell me of crucial tea and sit downs where love has taken root and blossomed over a pack of HobNobs. This is important because whipping out your HobNobs for just anybody could be misinterpreted as coming on a bit strong. If you are not after forming a relationship with whoever you are flashing your biscuits at, it's best to come right out with it, rather than cause an unpleasant scene later.

The HobNob quickly rose to become one of McVitie's' most important lines, and has found itself on the cutting edge of new developments. The tube, a small self-contained cardboard biscuit barrel with polythene lid, was pioneered by the Chocolate HobNob and stablemate the Milk Chocolate Digestive. Hobnobs are also now available in mini-packs, as the core of chocolate biscuit bars, and, turning full circle, smashed up and added as an ingredient to Flapjacks. Perhaps the success of the HobNob played its part in the waning popularity of the Abbey Crunch. If that is true then perhaps the HobNob should have a little ceremony each year when it observes a minute's silence, remembering the biscuits that went before so that it might enjoy the freedom and liberty of the oats section on supermarket shelves.

⟨13⟩ Sandwich Biscuits

Take two biscuits, place them back to back with a blob of something in between and you have a sandwich biscuit. This basic sandwich design has a lot of things going for it: most importantly, you are effectively eating two biscuits at once, and in any social situation where you don't want to be seen as a selfish biscuit glutton, a few well-chosen sandwich biscuits are going to maximise your handful. Additionally, the laminated construction results in a composite material that allows them to stand up to stresses and strains quite well. This can be important for extended dunking experiments or when building little piles of them on plates.

Bourbon

I fear I am going to create controversy here. My views on the Bourbon biscuit are somewhat similar to my feelings towards Jennifer Lopez. When described to the uninitiated, both sound lovely and each is greatly admired. I, however, find myself somewhat underwhelmed. I often feel that I'm missing the point with the Bourbon biscuit, and by rights I should like it a lot more than I do. Though it frequents a great number of biscuit assortments, I often find that I will pass it over, often in favour of biscuits with apparently lesser charms.

I can quite imagine that some people think that a Bourbon is about as good as it gets. I'm just not one of them. Nevertheless, I still have a great deal of respect for it, being as it is one of the elder statesmen of the biscuit tin, and it can certainly show the Johnny-come-lately biscuits a thing or two about classic biscuit design.

Why it should be named after a sixteenth-century French–Italian royal dynasty is anybody's guess. When faced with such historical conundrums there is really only one way forward for the semi-diligent biscuit critic, and that is to fabricate some weak theory. Let's say that Charles II of Bourbon

liked a plate of chocolate sandwich creams as he conquered the crowns of Naples and Sicily and restored them to a united and independent kingdom.

The one shown here is a Crawford's Bourbon, also well known for their Custard Creams. As you can see, these Bourbons have excellent embossing and the regulation ten holes, and you can clearly make out the little sugar crystals embedded in it. There is good sport to be had in breaking Bourbons apart to get at their chocolate cream filling, with points being scored for precision and full marks going to complete removal of the cream as a single entity.

Bourbons are also reassuringly uniform in size, regardless of the manufacturer: 61mm by 31mm being the accepted standard. Given their regular dimensions, perhaps Bourbon biscuits could form the basis of an SI unit of measurement, with biscuits being measured in Bourbons: for example, the digestive has a diameter of 1.13 bourbons, or that ocean liner over there is 7.6 kilobourbons long, or the wavelength of light emitted by that Krypton laser is approximately 46.1 nanobourbons. I'm sure you see what I'm getting at.

Custard Cream

When Hollywood wanted a time machine to carry Michael J. Fox around, not only did they decide to make it out of a sports car, but they plumped for plutonium, lightning and nuclear fusion as its power sources. If the British ever build a time machine then not only would it resemble some form of comfy chair but my betting is that it will have at its core a twin pack of Custard Creams. This biscuit, perhaps more than any other, has the ability to warp the fabric of space–time and transport us effortlessly back to days gone by. This is particularly impressive as a recent TV programme I saw about time machines said that it's the ones that go backwards in time that are the trickiest to build.

The Custard Cream was actually the first true adult biscuit that I tackled, back in the mid–1960s, as a small baby. Actually, I wasn't small, I was huge: about the size of a Mini, judging from Nanny Nicey's old photos. Before then I had been developing nascent biscuit-munching skills on Bickiepegs, a specially designed teething biscuit for babies. Bickiepegs, which are still available today, are possibly the hardest substance for ingestion that can be bought over a chemist's counter. When I tried one recently, it was a bit like gnawing on an everlasting wholemeal super-strength bread stick. It took twenty-five minutes just to blunt one end. After going up against a Bickiepeg, you simply have to view teething babies with a great deal of respect and caution.

Stepping up from the Bickiepeg to the Custard Cream made quite an impression on me. Having been told by several of Nanny Nicey's cohorts what an objectionable little chap I used to be, it was a very rare occasion indeed when somebody would actually find themselves in the unenviable position of babysitting me. On one such occasion my Aunty Edna quickly established that feeding me the filling from Custard Creams had a calming effect upon me: this no doubt contributed to my life-

long interest in the subject of biscuits. Even today, I find it difficult not to resist prising open the two halves and scoffing the filling. In general, the cream always adheres more strongly to one biscuit than the other, and it's this one which often bears the tell-tale twin furrows, where it has been de-creamed using the front two upper incisors.

With its baroque detailing, the Custard Cream defies us to pin it down to any particular period of history. It is tempting to think that it was knocking around in the sixteenth century, its ornate swirls providing the muse for such great artists as Rubens or Caravaggio, as they nibbled on one over a late morning cuppa. It is equally at home in any decade of the twentieth century and now through into the twenty-first.

Perhaps Custard Creams habitually transport themselves through time and we are simply unaware of it. The ones in your biscuit tin could be exchanging themselves with a pack from some time during the 1950s and you'd never know. But what would a time machine based on the Custard Cream look like? Taking our design cues from the biscuit, then it looks like it is going to need a set of ornate wrought-iron gates, front and back. It also needs a large diamond shape on the front with the words 'Time Machine' written in the middle. However, the filling or passenger area must not resemble custard in any discernible way, apart from being opaque and quite sweet. There would probably need to be a small travel kettle in there as well, a bit like the ones you get in hotel rooms.

Actually, talking of hotel rooms, the Custard Cream, in the form of a three-pack, can often be found next to the complementary tea and coffee and should be consumed within five to ten minutes of first entering the room, even prior to figuring out how the TV remote works. I have always thought that hotels should make it very clear which type and how many complementary biscuits they provide. Maybe on their signs, underneath their various stars and ratings, they could have a small weatherproof fac-simile of the biscuit selection on offer. I for one would find that helpful.

 # Jam

Just looking at the word 'jam' tells us how important it is. All the really fundamental words have three or four letters: 'man', 'cat', 'pot' and 'car'. Why the Americans persist on calling cars 'automobiles' is beyond me. Are they making a rod for their own back? Of course, you can only really effectively rhyme 'wheel' with 'automobile' in song lyrics which is why songs about cars were in danger of stalling at the works of Chuck Berry. After that, American writers were forced to start using brand names like 'Cadillac' in their songs. By contrast, the British were able enjoy the Beatles' 'Drive my Car', Madness's 'Driving in my Car' and Gary Numan's 'Cars'.

Now jam is pretty terrific stuff all by itself. In fact, younger readers would cheerfully eat it with a spoon if allowed. In the world of biscuits, cakes and puddings, jam has always been available to bring a bit of fruit-based interest and often plays an important structural role, acting as an all-purpose adhesive. Pectin from the fruit sets the jam and determines how stiff it is. When heated and cooled, it forms a big tangled mass which holds the jam together, but still allows it some movement: if it weren't for pectin, jam would be either a drink or a boiled sweet.

Jammie Dodger

A modern-day jam classic, the Jammie Dodger is made by Burton's Biscuits, producers of a wide range of biscuits but best known for their highly individual brands like Toffypops, Wagon Wheels and Viscount, all iconic brands in their own rights.

Like myself, Jammie Dodgers are a child of the sixties and have been made in Burton's Llantarnam factory in South Wales ever since they were introduced. Output runs at twelve biscuits a second, which is quite brisk, but we are still looking at around seventy years before achieving lunar orbit. However, if Burton's used some of their jam to stick the biscuits together then it might not be the fastest biscuit to the moon, but it could well be the best constructed.

Conceptually simple, a Jammie Dodger is a sandwich of jam and two shortcake biscuits with a heart-shaped hole in the upper biscuit to reveal the jam. The jam is billed as raspberry flavour but is in fact made from plums and a few other things, presumably because actual raspberry jam wasn't up to the biscuit-engineering task of adhering the two biscuits together. The biscuit itself has undergone some changes over the years. It has become somewhat paler in colour, and with this slightly softer. Also, the original heart-shaped embossing has been replaced by 'jammie' splashes so as to emphasise to the eater that jam plays a pivotal role in this biscuit.

Despite its relative youth, the reason why a Jammie Dodger is so called have mostly been forgotten. I think the explanation is to be found in a nursery rhyme:

> The Queen of Hearts,
> She baked some tarts,
> All on a summer's day.
> The Knave of Hearts,
> He stole the tarts,
> And took them clean away.

Jammie Dodger packs used to feature the Knave of Hearts, and to this day the heart-shaped jam hole echoes the past. I assume the Knave had to do some dodging, in the manner of Dickens' Artful Dodger, in order to carry out the theft. (By the way, tart baking seems like a very domestic pastime for royalty to be involved in. And baking during the heat of a summer's day is possibly going to lead to personal hygiene issues for Her Majesty, especially if she is wearing her full Queen outfit.)

A recent innovation has been the Mini-Jammie Dodger, which sees yet another old faithful following a trend seen across both biscuits and confectionery. Making smaller versions of something has long equated with 'fun', as pioneered by Mars. Of course, it has its place, but I think I'll always prefer seriously big, rather than little and fun. Perhaps it is because I remember my first encounter with the Jammie Dodger at the school tuck shop in 1971, where one of these substantial biscuits could be bought for two pence.

Jam Cream Sandwich

A common mistake is to call a Jam Cream Sandwich biscuit a Jammie Dodger. This is akin to calling all vacuum cleaners 'Hoovers', and it's perfectly fine to pour scorn upon anybody who makes this mistake. No, honestly, go ahead: people have to learn. For many, the Jam Cream Sandwich is the pinnacle of jam biscuitry. Normally such biscuits are to be found in assortment tins with their numbers strictly regulated to single figures, making them highly prized. However, most supermarkets now sell their own-label packs of fifteen, so you can go mad and potentially get your hands on quantities running into the hundreds.

The first thing that strikes you about these biscuits is their relatively small diameter. Straight away, you know that you'll need at least three just to get the measure of them. Sticking both halves of the biscuit together is a team effort between the jam and cream, with the jam occupying the bit below the hole. Separating the two halves is easy as the jam is quite pliable, typically being made using actual raspberries. Pulling the biscuits gently apart creates a small well in the jam, a bit like one of those visualisations of the gravity field around a black hole. If you don't know what I mean just imagine a small well. Yes, with a bucket if you like. A traditional dusting of granulated sugar on top of the sticky jam completes the picture.

Osmosis

Jam has been made throughout the ages by boiling fruit, a little water and, when it became available, sugar. The sugar in the fruit acts as a natural preservative once it becomes concentrated enough, and acts through a process called osmosis.

Osmosis is one of those words that people tend to bandy around without knowing what it actually means. It's specifically the diffusion of water molecules from an area of high concentration to one of low concentration. This is made possible if the solutes, the stuff dissolved in the water, are prevented from moving by some sort of barrier. This is exactly how jam works at the molecular level and means that water molecules that are free to move from anything landing on the jam will do so. Bacteria and fungi cells that land on jam have all of their life-giving water sucked from them, causing the naughty little unicells to implode. This helps stop the jam from going bad and gives rise to its alternative name of 'Preserve'.

So when you hear people say something flowery like, 'Oh, he learnt to play the guitar by osmosis really', what they are actually saying is that water diffused into him despite his skin having evolved since the time of the first reptiles to prevent this. Not only that, but the water conferred upon him musical ability. Of course, if the guitar was in a solution that he swallowed then the water could have been taken up by the lining of the gut. It's all fairly unlikely, and at best a very poor metaphor.

Happy Face

Jacob's Happy Face is a shining example of a jam and cream sandwich biscuit. A very good sign is that the pack has little pictures of raspberries all over it and, yes, it is real raspberry jam, no apples and plums in disguise. You can certainly taste the difference. The effect of the filling being viewed through the eyes and mouth of the face creates teeth and eyelids. The picture on the front of the pack is a little off in this regard as the faces have top teeth rather than bottom teeth. The biscuits themselves, 45mm in diameter, are simple smooth shortcake type of affairs, which hold their face graphics well enough. Altogether we have observed five types of face, which is very good going for a pack of ten biscuits.

A little while ago while waiting to do a spot of TV I found myself sitting next to a wine 'expert' from the US, who was of the opinion that it was a lot of hoo-ha that wine should be drunk at the correct temperature, allowed to breathe, and so on. I have to say that being surrounded by a studio of food and drink lovers, this chap's theories were met with some very stony faces. When it comes to biscuits, ask any Aussie and they will tell you that Tim Tams are best eaten fresh from the fridge. As for the Happy Face, it would seem to suit a fairly warm environment as its jam is liable to become a bit glassy at low temperatures, even snapping in two when bitten. It can also break away from the biscuits completely, leaving you with just a lump of jam to chew, which admittedly is no bad thing. When the jam is pliable, however, the whole biscuit works in concert, and is very good indeed.

Marshmallow Sort of Things

Biscuit bakers have lots of construction materials available to them which they can use to create new and interesting designs. One of the most whimsical of these is marshmallow, which can be used to add colour, texture and precise amounts of 'squidginess' to biscuits. The small band of biscuits that have opted for marshmallow fixtures have formed an elite group, both widely revered and often misunderstood. Having a marshmallow is often seen as a sign of immaturity in a biscuit, and marshmallow biscuits often find themselves on duty at children's parties or occasionally at a family picnic. This is a great shame as they have so much more to offer than that.

I would like to see a new dinner course invented that brings these noble and fluffy treats in from the cold, taking their rightful place alongside cheese and crackers or after-dinner mints. Actually, I think the Scottish may have already done this with their high tea, a hybrid of afternoon tea and a conventional high tea. A Scottish high tea has a course for scones, cakes, biscuits and teacakes in which our marshmallow-based biscuits are afforded the proper deference.

Marshmallow manifests itself in two distinct forms: the most common of these contains gelatin. Gelatin, a protein, is the stuff which sets jellies, and it is an animal product. Various people, such as vegetarians, avoid gelatin: for those who choose to consume it, this can be a handy way of warding such people off your biscuits. In fact, you can pretend that even stuff that doesn't have gelatin is loaded with it. Conversely, fairly dire biscuits that people have brought back from Spanish holidays can be palmed off on mildly desperate vegetarians as being totally free of gelatin (mind you, they might be full of whale oil and veal, so if you have a shred of conscience you might want to check for that with your Spanish-to-English dictionary).

Marshmallows with gelatin can be thought of as a foamed-up jelly or, put another way, a stiff jelly full of air. The other form of marshmallow is essentially an uncooked meringue, in which egg white or albumen is beaten with sugar, again to trap air. Such 'mallow' is very sticky indeed and has properties somewhere between bath sealant and shaving foam. I'm in constant awe of the factories that manage to handle this stuff in a directed and deliberate way for the purposes of biscuit production. Given just a tiny amount, the younger members of staff are able to lay waste to entire dining tables and sets of clothes.

I often wonder what would happen if we were required to handle marshmallow on an industrial scale, say for an experimental run of biscuits. I'm sure it would quickly lead to a bakery equivalent of the Chernobyl disaster: one vast gungy white mess with bits of bakery stuck in it. Enormous and heroic helicopters would be needed to drop tons of concrete on the site, risking almost certain adhesion in the process. Vast sheets of thin aluminium foil with attractive little patterns on them would also be required to wrap it up to protect future generations.

Wagon Wheel

The Wagon Wheel is another biscuit-based wonder from that iconic biscuit maker, Burton's. If biscuits were music then Burton's would have a big foothold in the Glam Rock section, with such wonderful and individual biscuits as the Jammie Dodger, Toffypop and the Wagon Wheel. Loved by kids and adults alike, Wagon Wheels create an instant sense of nostalgia. Perhaps more than any other biscuit, it has a rich and intriguing history, so much so that some of it has passed into the realms of urban myth.

The Wagon Wheel traces its origins back to the 1950s and a biscuit baron called Garfield Weston. An entrepreneurial Canadian, he made a fortune out of supplying biscuits to the forces during the war and had a facility in Slough. Mr Weston had three sons. One inherited the UK business, one had the Canadian, and the third got Australia. To this day, the Wagon Wheel can be found in these three locations. The brainchild of Garry Weston, the UK son, they were originally sold in the UK as Weston's Wagon Wheels.

If we look at today's UK Wagon Wheel then we find ourselves on familiar ground. Originally they were supplied in boxes of four as two stacks of two with a brown plastic tray keeping them in order. Individually wrapped since the 1980s, today the wrapped versions are again arranged in stacks of two to make eight-and six-packs. The individual wrap also allowed Wagon Wheels to venture into new territories such as canteens and cafés, not to mention the all-important lunchbox, rubbing shoulders with such experienced practitioners as the Penguin and Club.

The original packaging featured cowboys and gingham cloth, and this endured for many years. The designs then changed quite a bit, at one point even having American footballers on them, but Burton's eventually returned to their roots. Today's pack features a wagon train image with the strapline 'A Taste for Adventure', which becomes progressively less clear the more you think about it.

The Wagon Wheel has always been a bit of a conundrum, because if we consider its components in turn, it's puzzling why we like them at all. Its unique chocolate-flavoured coating, apparently called 'Blackpool coating', gives the Wagon Wheel a strange grey vinyl silk sheen, reminiscent of the bloom on ripe wild fruits. It forms a tortured mass of ripply bumps on the surface, almost as if it's not meant to be there at all and has managed to adhere to the surface despite the odds. As for what it tastes like compared to chocolate, who knows? The largest deposits are to be found in the gully formed where the two biscuits meet. You might just be able to pick out a big enough bit of it to tell what it tastes like in isolation.

Now on to the marshmallow centre. Its main role is to provide an interesting structural layer, allowing both biscuit layers a degree of independent horizontal movement once the flimsy chocolate seal has been compromised. As for what it tastes like in isolation, again, I doubt if anybody knows for sure. Finally, there are the two biscuit layers themselves. Your guess is as good as mine as to what is happening there. They seem to be a bit like a vaguely pliable thin shortcake biscuit. Research leads me to believe that they are a type of Marie biscuit, but I find it hard to believe.

However, put all of these unique things together, as Burton's have, and something magic happens: you get the compelling whole that is the Wagon Wheel. In some form of biscuit synergy the whole is far greater than the sum of its parts.

Other taste variants have come and gone, including a malted milk-based version called 'Big Country', which may have been all the reason the late Stuart Adamson needed to leave Scottish punk rockers the Skids and form the bagpipe-guitar-sound band with the same name. Later, 'Big Country' would be replaced by an excellent Toffee Wagon Wheel, which had a reservoir of runny toffee engineered into it. Regrettably this too is now just a memory but the jam version is still going strong and in fact is the default version in both Australia and Canada.

A few years ago Wifey and I enjoyed a Wagon Wheel bonanza when our friend Emma provided us with two forty-eight-packs of Toffee and Jam Wagon Wheels. Her dad ran an intermittent sandwich round and the Wagon Wheels were languishing in his lock-up, looking for a good home. I can honestly say that I was sorry to finish them and hadn't grown the least bit sick of them. I'm unsure if this is a plus for the Wagon Wheel or a minus for myself. It's also said that when the Soviet Union broke up at the end of the Cold War, lots of Wagon Wheels were discovered in the KGB's headquarters. If you ever have Mr Putin round for tea you know what to whip out after the trifle.

HAS THE WAGON WHEEL GOT SMALLER?

No discussion of the Wagon Wheel can be complete without reference to the perennial 'Has it got smaller?' question. Burton's are quick to dismiss this with the plausible explanation that the reduction in size of the Wagon Wheel is due to our childhood memories recalling a biscuit that was relatively larger compared to us. If you ever visit your old junior school you will experience much the same thing as you tower over your old tables and chairs. It should be noted that this phenomenon doesn't appear to occur with other large-diameter biscuits such as the Digestive, but then they probably didn't have such an impact on our impressionable young minds.

It does seem logical that if each successive generation of biscuit eaters since the 1950s had witnessed a real and substantiated shrinking then by now the Wagon Wheel would be so small that we would need special equipment just to see it, let alone remove the wrapper. Burton's by association would have pioneered the now emerging field of nanotechnology, and we could all enjoy Wagon Wheels as some form of molecular spray applied to the back of the hand. There has, however, been one very minor and reported shrinkage some twenty years ago when production was moved from the original factory in Slough to a new site at Llantarnam. At this time a new and more efficient biscuit-cutting roller was introduced and this did away with the old scalloped edge. In doing so, it shaved a couple of millimetres off the biscuit.

Interestingly, the Australian Wagon Wheel still has the scalloped edge, like some living fossil, an echo of a distant age of giant biscuits. I recently ate a pack which was sent to me purely for research purposes. As I gazed upon it I felt like Doug McClure in *The Land that Time Forgot* when the pterodactyl is going for him. The Australian biscuit had a diameter which measured 88mm: that's a whole 14mm bigger than our version. However, the British version comes right back at its colonial cousin with a depth of approximately 15mm compared to 11mm. In fact, the Aussie Wagon Wheel has some of the thinnest mallow I've ever witnessed. I'm sure if NASA had to produce some sort of super-thin mallow-based biscuit for use in space, say as a solar sail, then they would be down to Australia like a shot.

Teacakes

The overlord of the Teacakes is the Tunnock's, which registers a Victoria plum, possibly a clementine, on the fruit and nut scale of measurement, intimidating its walnut-sized competitors. While on the subject of its competitors, they all seem to need intricate plastic trays to protect their puny chocolate shells, while the Scottish Tunnock's makes do with a bit of thin tin foil and a cardboard box.

The Tunnock is a classic example of the egg-based marshmallow Teacake. Yet again I'm still left wondering how exactly the famous Tunnock's factory in Uddingston, Glasgow, is still standing, working with such tricky materials. I'm sure if I asked Mr Boyd Tunnock nicely enough he would come and let me have a peep, but I think I actually prefer not to know. I'd rather construct vast Heath-Robinson Teacake-baking machines in my imagination. Nevertheless, somehow a biscuit base gets a generous dollop of sticky marshmallow, and then is entirely coated in chocolate. Finally we must note that the Tunnock's contains no jam, which I assume is a level of extra gunge that would push their machine into the realms of fantasy.

The other sort of Teacake is the generally smaller gelatin marshmallow-based variety. Brands to look out for here are Burton's and, from Scotland again, Lee's. Here the marshmallow offers enough structural integrity to fashion a small jam reservoir, and runny jam at that. This slightly smaller Teacake is seldom individually wrapped and prefers a custom-moulded tray insert as its packing.

With such an elaborate construction, there are many ways to deconstruct a Teacake during its eating. The first and most prized is the complete removal of the upper chocolate dome as a single intact entity. This exposes the marshmallow, which can be peeled off the base and then eaten. Finally the base itself may be consumed. Sometimes the chocolate shell needs to be cracked and removed in sections, which is obviously more time-consuming.

In circumstances where numbers of Teacakes per person are strictly rationed, this can prolong one's eating pleasure.

Kimberley

The marshmallow genre contains some of the most divisive biscuits. Like olives, you either love them or hate them. Half the world claim some sort of Irish lineage: if they really were then they would possess the genes that enable them to enjoy the Kimberley biscuit. As Irish as rain, followed by a big downpour and then some showers, the Kimberley is a keystone of Irish tea and sits downs, as much as Barry's tea is. Indeed, the importance of the Kimberley to Irish culture and the affection in which it is held have been impressed upon me by most Irish people wishing to educate me further. Irish folks travelling from their native land are genuinely shocked that the rest of the world doesn't have the Kimberley. The truth is that most of the world has never even heard of them.

When I heard of its faintly gingery biscuits enclosing a marshmallow centre encrusted with sugar, I thought, Yes, this is a biscuit I would like to track down and sample. So it came as somewhat of a shock to find that it tasted a bit like damp MDF with a squirt of bath sealant. I paused, shocked and alarmed, and gathered my taste buds. What could be going on here? Maybe they were more reminiscent of a pack of errant Digestives that had been carelessly left in the garden for a week? Still reeling, I checked to see if the packet was out of date, but found that it was good for another six months. The locals informed me that it is the nature of the Kimberley to be variable in its texture and that I had probably got a particularly soft batch. I think they were just trying to make me feel better, knowing full well that I lacked the correct complement of DNA to get the most out of them.

Undaunted I set out to find another packet, and soon happened across the rarer (and slightly frowned upon by the purists) chocolate-covered variety. The crust of sugar granules over the edge of the marshmallow centre had been completely replaced by a coat of real milk chocolate. Although not apparent from the outer box, each biscuit was individually wrapped, and upon eating I was delighted to find these extra layers of protection had given rise to a Kimberley that had a slight crumble to it. In all respects it was excellent, worthy of a place on the greater world stage of biscuits. In fact, they are really worth tracking down.

Jacob's Mikado

For many people the marshmallow biscuit that springs to mind at the head of the queue is the Mikado or Mallow. Jacob's is the leading baker of this style of biscuit, although there are many smaller bakeries which make their own versions, with different names and variations of colour.

The Mikado is classically associated with children's birthday parties, where it provides a staple source of marshmallow and jam. I always have reservations about the use of coconut in biscuits, which seems more of a nod towards dietary fibre content than flavour. In the Mikado, however, the tartness of the simulated raspberry jam (it's actually apple) keeps the coconut at bay. The biscuit base is quite soft, with a crunch nowhere to be found. But it manages to sport some grid-like biscuit graphics, so it does appear to have some sort of mechanical properties. The pink marshmallow is arranged in two rows, five blobs in each. So what is the overall effect of this teatime treat

technology? Well, it's possibly the closest thing in the biscuit world to a salad. Having said that, younger members of staff destroy their ration at an impressive rate and even ask nicely for more, so it appears that the Mikado has lost none of its party time magic.

It must be mentioned that there is another form of Mikado, which is a strange international affair, being a German-style snack developed in Japan and baked in France (see p.130). We acquire them for UK consumption on sorties to the continent. This is the level of international collaboration usually seen with the development of a fighter aircraft or space stations, so it's nice to see it in the world of biscuits.

I'm afraid to say that I was responsible for a misunderstanding Nicey had about the Kimberley–Mikado and Coconut Cream biscuit. The problem was that I was sure there was a biscuit with such a name. I can describe it and everything. It's one of those biscuits with a biscuit base, covered in mallow, then finished off with a little bit of coconut sprinkled on top. I used to have it at parties, and on special occasions like school holidays. I sought one out for Nicey, who, being English but brought up in Wales, had never heard of it. It didn't take long to find one, probably in a garage somewhere, and I wasn't put off by the fact that it was just called a Mikado. I simply thought, Well, it's England, they probably just couldn't be bothered to give it its full title. Anyway, Nicey reviewed it as the 'Kimberley–Mikado', and my error soon became apparent as we were deluged by emails from 'proper' Irish people who obviously ate more biscuits than I was allowed to in childhood. The truth of the matter was that the Kimberley, the Mikado and the Coconut Cream were three very separate biscuits. My memories were obviously tainted by too much Guinness over the years. That, and a very catchy jingle that was played a lot on Northern Irish television that went, 'Kimberley, Mikado and Coconut Cream, someone you love, would love some, Mum!' Great advert: shame I thought it was all one biscuit and never tried the other two.

 # Fruity

Fruit. You can put it in a bowl and paint its picture, you can make it into salads or batter it flat, dry it out and stick it in biscuits. Could this crude explanation be the reason why melons aren't a familiar biscuit ingredient?

Fig Rolls

A lot of people tend to think of the Fig Roll as quite an outdated biscuit. I'm not actually sure why as they are just as relevant now as they have always been. Today we have many wonders: superglue, the interweb, Teflon, geo-synchronous communications satellites, extra-absorbent kitchen towels that stay strong even when wet, and the Fig Roll, which combines all the goodness of figs with the convenience of conventional biscuits.

I've often thought that the Fig Roll is as close to spaceman food as the biscuit world has ever got. I've never subscribed to that old science-fiction chestnut that in the future we'll all simply swallow a couple of nutrient pills and a glass of water instead of eating proper food. I, for one, find pills difficult to swallow, and it takes between three and four attempts for me to deal with a paracetamol, much to Wifey's disgust. In space, I would happily make do with just a couple of sandwiches, a cup of tea and five or six biscuits, insisting that all the little pills were saved for those who were really hungry.

After a hard morning working in space (realigning, say, your errant AE45 module) you're going to be fairly ravenous. You'll be wanting a decent biscuit and a cuppa, not some simulated little mid-morning snack-pill thing. Of course, what constitutes a morning's work will be subject to 'time dilation' as predicted by Einstein's laws of spacial relativity and caused by the immense interstellar velocities at which you'll no doubt be travelling. What seems like a morning's work for you could be a mere ten minutes. Actually, come to think of it, I'm sure I've seen the same thing occur in conventional terrestrial offices.

In space, Fig Rolls would be the perfect snack. I'm sure you could live on them for months and that their high-density and non-crumbly nature would lend itself to use in the space programme. Their sticky figgy filling makes them ideally suited to zero or micro gravity operating environments, as it helps stop stray bits of crust detaching and getting lodged in any sensitive or safety-critical systems. They are also high in fibre and complex carbohydrates, and would probably help with those all-important and tricky zero-gravity bathroom visits. No doubt if we ran into other space-faring alien races they'd have crates of alien Fig Rolls stashed away in the backs of their spaceships. Although it might take months or even years of effort by our best linguists before we work out enough of their alien tongue to ask them where they keep their Fig Rolls, or even if they have biscuits as we understand them.

Mind you, I also like to imagine that the Fig Roll was well known to the ancients, who were no strangers to the fig. Let's face it, back then puddings were a bit basic to say the least, the Black Forest Gateau or banoffee pie were unknown, so a few figs would probably have been about the size of it. I expect that the Egyptians built massive plantations all along the River Nile to satisfy their fig appetites. The Greeks, on the other hand, probably captured Phoenician fig ships in mad Jason and the Argonauts-style vessels, taking all the figs home for enormous fig parties. The historical evidence relating to the Roman Empire, meanwhile, is clear. Emperor Augustus, as played by Brian Blessed in the BBC production of *I Claudius*, loved a good fig, so no need to consult the history texts there.

I have heard it said that the Fig Roll is one of the oldest forms of sweet biscuit made in Britain. I don't know who said it, but it is entirely plausible. The Americans are under the impression that they created the whole genre in 1891, when baker James Henry Mitchell invented a machine for stuffing one lot of squidgy stuff inside something else equally pastry-like. They settled on fig jam as the middle bit, and named them Newtons after a nearby suburb of Boston.

There are two forms of Fig Roll – 'bake then cut' and 'cut then bake' and each has its merits. The Jacob's Fig Roll is perhaps the best-known example of cut then bake. They used to have ridges on the top, which was no good as it appeared to alter the fig-to-crust ratio, and these have now been sensibly removed. The cutting and baking process also gives them a distinctive slight curvature, which makes them less than straightforward to package. Various arrangements of plastic trays with no more than about three or four biscuits per compartment are used. Cut then bake Fig Rolls typically will have the pastry crimped at each end, which goes some way to sealing in the moist fig contents. As well as making them better citizens of the biscuit tin, this means that the nature of the fig filling cannot be easily assessed through a casual glance. Such Fig Rolls have an air of mystery due to their concealed innards, and upon first encountering them it is a little like unwrapping a surprise present.

Bake then cut Fig Rolls, on the other hand, are much more candid. As the continuous strip of biscuit leaves the oven it is cut to length. Each biscuit end is a cross-sectional study of the finished product. Nothing is left to the imagination and fig and crust may be compared in a single glance. The Fig Rolls also have a regular linear shape, which lets them stack neatly, and very impressive packing densities are possible. Such Fig Rolls come into their own when space is at a premium, such as Wifey's little rucksack which we use for picnics. Most of the own-label Fig Rolls in the UK are bake then cut, and are made by Burton's Foods.

One of the interesting aspects for the keen Fig Roll buyer is the variance in fig content from own-label to own-label, which can vary from a minimum of 20 per cent to a maximum of 30 per cent. In a perfect world there would simply be a dial on the side of the Fig Roll production line by which the desired fig content could be selected. I can't help but picture imaginary designs for the workings of Fig Roll extruding machines in my head. I also like to imagine high-powered biscuit executives thrashing out business deals relating to fig percentages, hopefully while wearing enormous *Dallas*-esque Stetsons.

Garibaldi

There can be few biscuits as unique as the Garibaldi. Technically it's a semi-sweet hard fruit biscuit, but that description really doesn't do justice to this unparalleled teatime treat. They are often affectionately known as 'dead fly' or 'squashed fly' biscuits due to their payload of little flattened raisins. This name is sometimes also used for the Fruit Shortcake, which has a cargo of currants, but personally I don't hold with that.

With Garibaldi, a layer of raisins is squashed between an upper and lower sheet of biscuit dough, and here and there the odd raisin pokes through. The biscuits are finished with a shiny but non-sticky glaze (egg, I presume) which gives them a high specular index (important to know for anybody wishing to make a three-dimensional computer model of a Garibaldi). The biscuits are cut into rectangular slabs, each of which consists typically of five biscuits. Scoring made before baking leaves the biscuit equivalent of perforations in a sheet of raffle tickets.

I can't think of another biscuit that ships in this partially completed kit form. Conceivably you could just pick up one enormous slab and start gnawing on the corner but this would surely be the height of poor etiquette, and not as much fun. The skill in breaking up the Garibaldi slab is to achieve nice rectangular biscuits. Success depends on the subcutaneous raisin distribution, but even if you end up with some hopelessly odd shapes it doesn't matter. Where Garibaldis are concerned it's the taking part that matters, rather than the taking apart. As with any biscuit that has suffered some form of disfigurement, the kindest thing to do is to put the little chaps out of their misery, quickly and painlessly, using hot tea.

The most famous Garibaldi in history, apart from the bald bloke in *Babylon Five*, was undoubtedly the Italian revolutionary, Giuseppe. He spent a large part of the nineteenth century up to all sorts of warfare but is best known for trying to unify the various states, city states and kingdoms of Italy. People often ask if the biscuit was named after this Garibaldi, and I say, 'Yes, sure, why not.' It's claimed that to sustain his fighting force of Redshirts, Garibaldi's cooks came up with the compact and energy-rich biscuit. Having tucked away a few Garibaldis, they were all set up to invade Naples. Personally, I think I would need at least half a packet for a job of that size, as I can quite easily see off five or six after mowing the lawn. I suppose it's lucky that the biscuit wasn't called a 'Redshirt'.

During the 1970s a chocolate-covered variant of the Garibaldi could be found in some supermarkets, and those who recall this biscuit are still vainly searching the aisles a quarter of a century later. I encountered the chocolate-covered Garibaldi only once, but I remember it clearly. It was at a village fête that we visited, late one summer's afternoon. A tea and cake stall was selling them, and my dad knew we could not pass up this particular opportunity. Due to my limited exposure to the biscuits, I couldn't say if they were manufactured that way or if they had been created by the lady running the stall from biscuits and her own melted chocolate. Looking back, I assume it was the latter but either way they were utterly fantastic.

Fruit Shortcake

Pure class in a biscuit, the Fruit Shortcake delivers a great deal of punch for a mid-range biscuit, which is often even seen as a low-end biscuit. The clever distribution of fruit and a topping of sugar granules ramps up the sugar content to make this quite unlike any of its shortcake-based cousins: the unwary biscuit eater may easily work their way through half a packet of these beguiling little biscuits before they realise it. The edge detail and the patterning on the back also serve to give this biscuit an almost frilly, harmless look that is very disarming, and again can lead to very high numbers of biscuits being consumed.

Of course, any biscuit that is crusted with sugar in this way will tend to condition us to find such things appealing. I have big problems at our local builders' merchants with the sheets of forty-grit sandpaper, which produce a sort of Pavlov's dog response, my mind turning to large sugary baking-sheet-sized biscuits. It's a good job they don't print a raisin pattern on the paper or I don't think I would be able to resist a nibble.

 # Icing

Icing is a gloriously lo-tech way of making biscuits sweeter. Simply mix sugar with water to make a paste and spread it on top. Sometimes icing has some baking soda and acetic acid added to it that fizzes away to create little bubbles of carbon dioxide, making for a light and crispy, if slightly vinegary, shell. Children especially understand the value of icing as it is a crude form of 'sweets', and will set about picking it off the underlying biscuit, no matter how impractical this is.

Iced Gems

It is 1850 and in the town of Reading, Berkshire, emerging biscuit giant Huntley and Palmer is experimenting with some new biscuit technology. However, the new biscuits emerge from the oven having actually shrunk. But Thomas Huntley likes the resulting mini-biscuits, which are christened Gems, and they sell well. Sixty years later the company added icing and from hereon children's birthday parties would be incomplete without them. Now made in Liverpool, there are very few biscuits that can trace their origins back 150 years, and which everybody can remember from their childhood, even if they have just had their telegram from the Queen.

I have to say that it was with a certain amount of trepidation that I recently decided to revisit the Iced Gem after a thirty-year gap. I've always pictured them as a sort of sweetened gravel. There have been some changes to the Iced Gem since I last had them: however, these seem to be mainly confined to the icing, which is no bad thing. Today's Iced Gems come in five main colours and flavours — white, yellow, orange, red and purple – and a chocolate version is also now available.

I also recall that the icing originally tasted of sugar and artificial blancmange-type flavours, and that there were some fairly lethal sharp points on the icing that could inflict minor havoc on the roof of one's mouth. So I don't know if I was happy or sad to see that the points have largely gone and that the icing actually has discernible flavours, slightly fruity ones at that. In fact, I really was put in mind of various berries, red-currants and blackberries. Anyway, a ten-point piping nozzle places the icing somewhere on the base and the vertical orientation of the biscuit is pot luck. The chances of getting a bag of entirely intact iced gems are remote, so there are lots of lumps of icing that can be eaten directly.

Just in case I was getting carried away, the biscuit base is still as dry and uninspiring as ever. Back in the late 1850s, things must have been pretty rough if just straight non-Iced Gems were a big hit. If we hopped in our time machine and went back to the mid-nineteenth century armed with a pack of Chocolate HobNobs or even just a simple Fruit Shortcake, no doubt we could produce sensory overload and stupefaction in the populace.

After my long absence, I did find myself mildly enjoying these little old biscuits, but I also strangely missed the puncture wounds in the top of my mouth. Needless to say, the younger members of staff devoured them with relish.

Party Rings

The primary mission of ring-shaped food is that it be briefly worn as a ring before being eaten. This in itself raises the potential to amuse, and when a shiny, hard icing topping is added you have something so enthralling that it graces events such as birthday parties and Sunday teas at your aunty's house. The Iced Ring was once a common sight: however, it suffered with its habitat being given over to the all-pervasive chocolate biscuit and now has been beaten back to its final stronghold as the Fox's Party Ring. Luckily the Party Ring is a splendid example of the genre, having brightly coloured icing with feathered details.

There is an advert on telly right now where a lady has strange food-related hallucinations. The cushions next to her on the settee turn into big slices of sponge cake and the rug becomes a large puddle of chocolate in which she starts to sink in the manner of someone drowning in quicksand. As a portent against bad interior design the patterns on her wallpaper turn into a flock of Iced Rings which fly across the room, just missing her head. You would have thought that she would be well advised to find out who has been spiking her hot chocolate with mescaline. But no, it appears that she merely needs to eat a small portion of a specific type of chicken korma ready meal to banish these disturbing visions. I would probably stay clear of cheese at bedtime as well, just to be on the safe side.

 **Wafers**

The wafer is one of the many varied techniques whereby the food industry persuades us to buy and consume air. Prawn crackers are another, but at least the prawn cracker alerts the casual consumer to stay vigilant by bearing little relation to an actual prawn. In fact, if a prawn cracker ever encountered a prawn alive, dead or stir-fried, the prawn's surface moisture would inflict terrible soggy lesions upon the cracker, causing it to release tiny and harmless quantities of air. In an all-out fight between even a medium-sized prawn and a prawn cracker, my money would be on the prawn every time.

Pink Wafer

I like to think that I'm a fairly even-handed sort of chap when it comes to biscuit appraisal. After all, there is no need for spiteful comments or cheap jibes aimed at biscuits plying an honest trade, asking only of you that you eat them. One person's poison is another's pleasure, and the very reasons we might cite for detesting something may be the very reasons why somebody else adores it. However, when it comes to pink wafers, that all goes out the window.

Mostly, with such dreadful old biscuits, a simple mutual understanding is all that is needed: I won't bother you if you don't bother me. I had come to just such an arrangement with the Lemon Puff, whose tangy lemon cream, while stimulating, could never compensate for its cracker-box-reject taste. Still, I had a certain respect for its position. A sticky caramelised sugar glaze on the biscuit was futile and messy but it was at least individual. The scalloping around the edges of the rectangular biscuit also failed to add any real value, but merely provided more detritus to dislodge and get gummed under one's fingernails thanks to that sticky glaze. Yes, I may not have liked it, even thought it misguided and pompous, but after our initial falling out we steered clear of one another.

The Pink Wafer has never known such good grace, and takes every opportunity to parade its loathsome pink carcass. It doesn't even have the manners to keep itself to itself, frequently soiling nearby biscuits with tatty flakes shed from its miserable husk. It's not unknown for its corners to drop off, as if afflicted by some fearsome tropical disease. What could be less appetising than the biscuit version of the Singing Detective? I would prefer not to mention its cream filling, but for the sake of rigour let's quickly consider it. It really is nothing more than wafer adhesive, usually present in mere trace amounts. One enterprising manufacturer has stoked theirs full of vitamins and minerals, so you can get 10 per cent of the recommended daily intake of zinc from eating one. This is no doubt aimed at children, and concerned parents. Well, that's fine, if you intend relying on Pink Wafers as an integral part of your daily diet. I think I might just stick to eating lots of fresh vegetables.

By rights, the Pink Wafer should have been left to disintegrate safely inside its own packet. Alas, it appears that it has friends in high places, or at least in the places that decide on the contents of biscuit selection packs. Perhaps it is its ability to add air which is prized here. It can't be its appeal because the Pink Wafers are always the last to go. Perhaps that is because the Pink Wafer seems to be the most manufactured of all biscuits. There is simply no way that you are ever going to be able to knock up a tray of them using your gas cooker, or to capture that artificial flavour.

The final damning piece of evidence is the appearance from time to time of packs in 'pound' shops alongside the imitation cookware and gingham tea towels. I have seen an even more troubling sight in one such shop: *Green* Wafers. I can tell you no more than that due to the very wide berth I afforded them.

Baking your own biscuits is not a difficult thing to do. The recipes tend to be very simple, the ingredients relatively straightforward and most can be baked in under thirty minutes with results that are, as often as not, sublime. The aroma of a rack of biscuits hot from the oven is beyond compare.

At this point you might think that we are about to regale you with at least seven or eight of our favourite recipes. Well, no. The trouble is most of us simply can't be bothered. Let's face it, biscuits are for relaxing with. Who wants to spend an hour or more fussing around in the kitchen with weighing scales and a wooden spoon?

The answer is Americans, who like to bake their cookies. Given that most American kitchens seem to be the size of the average UK leisure centre, perhaps it's just a means of passing the time while they try to recall the route out of the rest of the house. However, they often resort to shop-bought ready-made cookie dough which just needs baking. This is an operation of about equal complexity to popping some deep-frozen sausage rolls in the oven. Mind you, if we were faced with supermarket shelves filled with Oreos we would feel compelled to bake our own biscuits, too.

Does Somebody Live There?

There is a wonderfully lazy way of getting hold of homemade biscuits without suffering the washing-up fallout from actually making them in your own home. Simply buy 'homemade' biscuits. I've often wondered how 'homemade' biscuits are made commercially. Even if Wifey and I spent eight hours a day baking biscuits in our

1960s Cannon gas oven (now converted to North Sea gas) I doubt whether we could produce enough to supply and support a national distribution chain. This is to say nothing of the amount of trips we would need to make to the supermarket to buy flour and so forth, or the strain it would place on our already ageing food mixer. So how do they do it? There are two possible answers.

🫖 **The manufacturers subcontract out the baking to a community of biscuit-baking homes.** This would probably work best if all the houses were on the same street or estate. Production could be scaled up by enrolling more streets into the production line, and could be streamlined by delivering all the raw ingredients as they pick up the finished homemade biscuits.

🫖 **The manufacturers get somebody to live permanently in their biscuit factory, thereby turning it into a home, and rendering anything made there 'homemade'.** For good measure they should also decorate, get some new curtains, a cat or dog and a real log fire, as these are often the things that turn a house into a home, and should work on an industrial unit or factory, too.

The most troubling moniker for biscuits is 'hand-baked', implying that individuals with incredibly hot hands cook the biscuits one at a time by cupping them in their hands. Alternatively they might just be grabbing a handful of biscuit mix and shoving it in the oven. Either way, it has to be a dangerous and probably unhygienic practice.

Tunnock's Wafer

On their own, wafers are pretty woeful specimens. They need to seek the help of other foodstuffs whenever possible to cover up the fact that they taste like mildly sweetened cardboard. Most gleefully accept their destiny as a glorified handle to a scoop of ice cream. The really lucky ones are reprieved, rehabilitated and end up inside a 'Tunnock's Real Milk Chocolate Caramel Wafer Biscuit'.

The Scottish have more experience of biscuit baking and the skilled deployment of sugar in biscuits and cakes than perhaps any other nation on earth. T. Tunnock Ltd of Uddingston, Glasgow, a family-run company that dates back to the 1890s, are a Scottish national treasure. The basic design of the Tunnock's Wafer consists of four layers of caramel sandwiched between five wafers. This is wrapped in a thin shell of actual milk chocolate. Each biscuit is clad in its own rectangle of foil and paper, adorned with distinctive red and gold stripes. Poet Laureate Ted Hughes was fond of scribbling short verses on the backs of Tunnock's wrappers, some of which he donated to the Tunnock's Caramel Wafer Appreciation Society of St Andrew's University. Apparently some in the society thought that he had committed a sacrilegious act and defiled the great wafer's wrapper, and as such weren't as impressed as no doubt they were supposed to be.

The wrapper bears the legendary and proud boast that 'More than 4,000,000 of these biscuits are made and sold each week'. Who eats this unrelenting tide of biscuits? That's the question that regularly crosses the mind of the casual Tunnock's eater. It was once assumed that the answer to this paradox lay with the Scots themselves. There are over 5 million of them. They should be able to take care of them all, even if they ate only one each a week. It has also been pointed out that the Scottish apparently enjoy a higher standard of healthcare than the rest of the UK. Maybe this helps certain individuals cope with massive intakes of Tunnock's wafers while strapped into advanced medical devices. I don't know for sure as this is pure speculation.

I was very happy to see the review eight-pack of wafers bearing the informative message 'Still original size'. It's wonderful to see a biscuit manufacturer taking such direct steps to address the issues that often trouble biscuit eaters.

recognisable, so much so that spotting a lesser-known variety was an event, of equal magnitude to seeing a Ford Escort in a colour other than pale blue. (Actually, at the height of the Club's powers, cars were painted in various sorts of metallic-effect brown, occasionally reminiscent of wooden fence panelling or fake tan, and this would be considered bad taste even in 1970s Britain.)

TV advertising featured a jingle so catchy that people would sing and hum it, for no good reason other than they liked to do so. Of course, if there actually was a bona fide reason, such as somebody mentioning the word 'club', then everybody would chime up in unison, 'If you like a lot of chocolate on your biscuit, join our Club'. The adverts featured various groups or clubs of individuals all singing the jingle, such as pensioners playing bowls and American footballers (I could well be making this up).

Unwrapping a Club was a series of personal preferences. First, slip off the outer paper tube, leaving it intact, or tug at its seam, opening it to form a small rectangular sheet. Then unwrap the foil-backed paper inner, either peeling the foil away from the paper or reforming the wrapper back into the shape of the biscuit. Personally, I liked to make two small origami dogs from the wrappers. Others rolled them into tubes or folded them over and over to make a minute and rather poor mirror.

Club biscuits are still available today but they have been entirely redesigned. This is the reason for my anguish, and I would appreciate it now if I could have a little time to myself. Thanks, I'll be all right in a minute or two.

Penguin

Take two cocoa-flavoured biscuits, sandwich some chocolate-cream icing between them, then coat lightly in chocolate. Finally, think of a name for your creation. In 1932, William McDonald, a biscuit manufacturer in Glasgow, did just that and decided that he should call his new creation 'Penguin'. This became a McVitie's brand when McDonald joined with McVitie's and Price, MacFarlane Lang and Crawford's to form United Biscuits in 1946. So if you think that you can't remember a time before Penguins you are probably right. Unless you are older than seventy, or you have lousy memory. Or perhaps you've never heard of them in which case I expect you're American and somebody British is forcing you to read this.

The Penguin is the flagship chocolate-covered biscuit bar of the mighty McVitie's, and has been the yardstick by which other chocolate-covered biscuits bars are measured. It pretty much created the now familiar 'chocolate count line' genre, whereby individually wrapped biscuits are sold by number rather than by weight. As we will see, it has been the inspiration for other biscuits which have gone on to become icons in their own right. It also had its imitators which had to be dealt with.

There are many people to whom it has occurred that the Penguin is nothing more than a chocolate-covered Bourbon biscuit. It's not. The texture of the biscuits is altogether different, being crisper and less dense. The chocolate-cream filling is also much paler. The covering of milk chocolate is quite thin and yet registers as the main ingredient. In the Penguin we see once again a biscuit that must be enjoyed as a whole, as analysis of its components does not convey its charm.

When I was little, Penguins were wrapped simply in three different-coloured wrappers: green, blue and red. Each had the minimal Penguin logo and they were identical save for the colour. Green ones were usually left to last as it was common knowledge to children that all green sweets or confectionery are in some way derived from washing-up liquid. Today's Penguin eaters are treated to lolly-stick-style jokes on the back of the wrapper, and pictures of penguins in a variety of amusing situations. I think the old foil wraps were better, much in the way that radio is better than TV, and books are better than radio, right back to no cave painting was better than cave painting. Anyway, with their seventy-fifth anniversary fast approaching, maybe United Biscuits could knock out a big batch of retro Penguins in the old wrappers. That would be the biscuit equivalent of driving a beautifully restored classic car. Or, even better, pick eight wrappers from the past and put them in the pack in chronological order, to form a little history lesson.

Penguin was one of the first biscuits to be advertised by name rather than company, so much so that the Penguin brand now forms an umbrella in its own right under which a recent slew of new products has been created. The Penguin itself is sometimes available in mint and orange flavours, but has kept its dignity thus far and resisted the urge to go mini or giant. Other products include cake bars, dipping pots, Chuckas (which are little pots of biscuit, chocolate and caramel pellets) and Splatz and Mini-Splatz (which appear to be re-engineered BN biscuits). I think there is enough continuity with the original Penguin to make a valid link but they stay far enough away from it so as not to erode its integrity. So, despite all this activity, Penguins have lost none of their self-esteem, which is no mean feat. Still, there is always the ice cream or breakfast cereal option available.

Perhaps one of the reasons for Penguin's appeal is its association with the emperor penguin. Penguins are one of nature's premium comedy birds, which is a bit of a coup, seeing as Guinness had already bagged the Toucan and the Ostrich. The famous 'P . . P . . Pick up a . . . Penguin' strapline is now confined to the packs; however, in the golden days of Penguin TV advertising a few shots of some penguins waddling around and the uttering of the catchphrase were all that was needed to deliver a memorable advert.

Penguin has had to defend its honour against those who would seek to pass themselves off as one. In 1997 Mr Justice Walker found in favour of United Biscuits (McVitie's), who were more than a little upset by UK supermarket chain Asda's Puffin biscuit. Asda had chosen to sail as close to the wind as they could with their packaging, so that consumers would know that they were offering a Penguin-like product. However, they went too far, and the combination of seabirds beginning with the letter P, its cartoon picture and the pack design landed them in court. As the learned judge so ably put it, 'Had the Asda product been called, for example, "Bison", to take another name from the original list, with a cartoon picture of a brown woolly bison on the packaging, these proceedings could not possibly succeed.' The case proved to be something of a landmark ruling for UK supermarkets, who have subsequently all backed off with their 'me-too' type products.

 # Foreign

Travel broadens the mind. It also teaches us that the rest of the world doesn't really have a clue about making decent biscuits, but why should they when they don't drink proper tea either? Occasionally there are glimmers of hope, but it's all a bit fleeting as they don't really understand why one biscuit might be better than another when it comes to teaming it up with a nice cuppa. Still, they muddle on in their own well-meaning way, so let's take a look at a few handpicked examples that offer some hope.

Tim Tam

In 1958 an Australian called Ian Norris, director of biscuit technology for Australian biscuit maker Arnott's, was on a world tour hunting for ideas. While in the UK he encountered the Penguin and as legend has it thought, That's not a bad idea for a biscuit . . . but we'll make a better one. On return to Australia he began work and five years later Arnott's launched the Tim Tam. The name was taken from the winner of the 1958 Kentucky Derby, attended by Ross Arnott, who thought the name perfect for their new biscuit. Of course, he may have had to think again if the outcome of the race had been different. Biscuit history could have been changed for ever if the third-placed 'Noureddin' or unplaced 'Red Hot Pistol' had triumphed.

The average Australian is a modest type, not in the habit of making overblown or exaggerated claims. However, they all seem confident in two things: that the Tim Tam is a work of perfection; and not to have eaten one is not to have truly lived. The UK and Australia have a common cultural heritage and are forever engaging in friendly rivalry in such areas as sport, music, low-budget TV soaps and blokes that annoy crocodiles (I'm sure we could find some lads who would do that: Bez from the Happy Mondays, for instance). So how does the Tim Tam stack up against its forbear, the Penguin; was Ian Norris right in thinking he had made a better biscuit?

First, the Tim Tam is quite a bit smaller and lighter than the Penguin, and its biscuit layers are seemingly closer to meringue or honeycomb than an ancestral Bourbon. It's this highly porous biscuit that enables the execution of the Tim Tam Slam, a messy pastime that I'll discuss in the following chapter on 'Dunking'. The tone of the two biscuits is also somewhat different: the Tim Tam is a warm bronze to the Penguin's almost slate-grey chocolate and biscuit. The more expensive Tim Tam has a buttery richness to both its chocolate and its chocolate cream. Arnott's actually describe their chocolate as having a caramel flavour. This all begins to make more sense when we consider that Arnott's markets the Tim Tam primarily to females between twenty and thirty-five, whereas the Penguin is aimed at the broader target of the family shopping basket. This is also reflected in their packaging: the individually wrapped Penguin can find its way into lunchboxes and sit alongside tills in cafés and shops, whereas the Tim Tam simply rests with its cohorts in a little plastic tray inside its outer wrapper. The Tim Tam has a rolling list of varieties, of which eight are available at any one time, with Original, Double Coat and Caramel forming the unchanging core. All the obvious bases are covered, such as Mocha, Dark Chocolate, White Chocolate, and Hazelnut, which seems to be a favourite Arnott's ingredient.

In an ironic twist, Tim Tams, like its mentor the Penguin, have had their own problems with 'me-tooism'. When the American food giant Campbell's added Arnott's to its portfolio, many Australians saw this as a threat to their much-loved biscuit heritage. No doubt as some form of protest, Australian entrepreneur Dick Smith saw this as a perfect opportunity to launch a virtually identical biscuit called the 'Tem-*p*-tin'. I got my hands on a pack and found the flavour to be not quite up to Tim Tam levels. Nevertheless Arnott's acted to protect its brand. They settled out of court and forced Dick Smith to make some changes. The troublesome, italicised '*p*' was Romanised, and the hyphens vanished altogether: the Tem-*p*-tin became Temptin. Maybe if he had called it 'Bison' he wouldn't have got into any trouble in the first place.

I see the Tim Tam and Penguin as two quite different biscuits in most respects. The Tim Tam is a classy little product, tastes great and its insubstantial nature affords the sucking of tea and coffee through it by Tim Tam Slammers such as Natalie Imbruglia. However, the mighty Penguin offers a more satisfying mouthful with a taste that has stood the test of time. There is something to learn from both biscuits and if you haven't tried one or the other then seek it out.

Euro-choc

Every year during the summer our music charts are invaded by saccharine and repetitive tunes from Spain, Germany and even, on occasion, Belgium. It's our own fault, of course: we hear them while on holiday with our guards lowered by sun and sangria. Once home a kind of withdrawal sets in and we look to prolong the suffering by demanding them from our local record shop. In this way another pan-European pop phenomenon is created. Then, at the end of September they become casualties of the first frosts of autumn, much like my French beans. So, does the same thing occur with biscuits? Not really, because by and large continental biscuits are pretty grim and misguided affairs.

There has been a long-running dispute between Britain and the rest of the EU concerning chocolate that dates back to 1973. An opt-out from European law allowed the UK (along with Ireland and Denmark) to continue to call our favourite brands 'chocolate', even though they contained milk or vegetable oil. The purists led by Belgium and France insisted that chocolate may only be called chocolate if it is made using solely cocoa butter for its fat content. In March 2000, it was decided that the simple addition of the word 'family' to describe UK products abroad as 'family milk chocolate' would do the trick. Before then, several UK governments had had to fend off Brussels' attempts to rename our chocolate 'vegelate' and even calling for an outright ban. So, with our blood boiling, let's look at Euro-choc, whatever that turns out to be.

Petit Beurre and Petit Écolier

The French Petit Beurre biscuit is one of those things that makes you question if you've grasped the rudiments of the French language. Does it mean 'little butter biscuit' in a cute sort of way? I incline to the other possibility – that they are made with a little butter – which would explain why they don't taste very buttery. If you want a buttery French biscuit, then get yourself a pack of Galettes Breton. They don't even mention butter in their name, but are really one of the best French biscuits I've encountered, with melt-in-the-mouth buttery tenderness. Perhaps there is some strange

Gallic inverted biscuit nomenclature. I must look out for *'sans absolutement les poissions et canards'* biscuits next time in the hypermarket.

It is an exceedingly French thing to combine bread and chocolate. There are numerous examples such as the 'pain au chocolat' and huge jars of chocolate spread for French bread. It was only a matter of time before somebody took a Petit Beurre and slapped a big old lump of chocolate on it. Leading French biscuit manufacturer LU did just that and called it, rather dubiously, a 'small schoolboy'.

On first encountering the Petit Écolier it appears bizarre, having embossed onto its slab of chocolate an odd-looking child carrying a basket. I think I ate my way through about four packs before I worked out that's what it was. You may also infer from that statement that no matter how much of a ribbing I'm about to deliver, they are actually quite tasty. On further investigation it turns out that the lad in question is called Jacques, son of poster artist Firmin Bouisset and painted by him in 1897. The baker and biscuit-maker LU adopted the image of the small schoolboy, originally pictured eating a straightforward Petit Beurre, over the even stranger image of a flying, trumpeting, laurel-distributing angel. Back in the nineteenth century, Jacques must have thought Petit Beurres were cutting-edge biscuit heaven. Nowadays they are ranked just below balsa wood, charcoal briquettes and airline food in the league table of appetising things to eat.

But back to the Petit Écolier. There is something decidedly disjointed about it: the chocolate and biscuit are very obviously created separately, then quickly fused together to create the finished item. While the edge of the slab is firmly attached, underneath gaps abound. I can appreciate the technical imperatives for this, but the result is a bit like eating a packet of Rich Teas while stealing bites off a block of milk chocolate. The overall effect is unsettling as it seems that the Petit Beurre has acquired the chocolate out of desperation, and indeed the slab may choose to up and leave if it gets a better offer, which seems likely.

Choco Leibniz

German bakers Bahlsen are perhaps best known in the UK for their Choco Leibniz, a refined chocolate slab with a biscuit stuck in it. Bahlsen, who were founded in Hannover in 1891, have biscuit bakeries in several European countries but none in the UK. As such the whole Bahlsen range is distinctively continental, which is to say it makes perhaps the most sense when viewed from over the brim of a coffee cup rather than a mug of tea.

The Choco Leibniz is a cult biscuit that enjoys a fiercely loyal following. This ensures that there is always a place for it in your supermarket. The base biscuit is essentially a German version of the Petit Beurre, renamed the Leibniz. I actually found it to be quite a pleasant little biscuit, with the butter flavour clearly present. These are available without chocolate or formed into animal-shaped biscuits to make Leibniz Zoo, which boast a particularly amusing penguin.

The Choco Leibniz prides itself on its unique construction, which involves filling moulds with melted chocolate. Just as the chocolate starts to set in goes the Leibniz biscuit, interesting side up. German engineering

ensures that there is excellent chocolate-to-biscuit bonding here, and no whimsical holes or gaps. The result is a biscuit that has an outer frill of chocolate and very fine detail in its chocolate relief. The first thing to do when eating one is to remove the chocolate frill with your incisors. Having done so, you can hold the biscuit securely without getting chocolatey fingers.

So rich is a Choco Leibniz that it can almost get caught around one's tonsils. I find it requires hot drinks to wash it down, or having experience of eating full-strength EU-sanctioned chocolate. Bahlsen tell me that people are most loyal to the plain chocolate version; however, when the product is in any sort of promotion the milk chocolate one takes the lion's share of sales. Once again we see the semi-fanatical plain chocolate crowd making their voice heard.

Oreo

Oh dear, oh dear. It's the biggest-selling biscuit on the planet and it doesn't even know it is a biscuit. The Oreo is baked across the world by Nabisco, the name being a contraction of 'The National Biscuit Company' of the USA. Like so many biscuits, the Oreo displays that innate quality

The word 'cookie' is derived from the Dutch word 'keokje' meaning 'little cake'. Clearly these aren't little cakes so that's slightly annoying. The word 'biscuit', by contrast, comes from the French words 'bis' and 'cuir', meaning literally twice-cooked. This refers to how biscuits used to be made back in the sixteenth century, for ship's rations. The simple dough was baked once to form the biscuit, and then received a long slow baking that dried it out as a form of preservation. The resulting 'hard tack' was then eaten with meals or ground up to make a fairly nasty sort of porridge. These biscuits were so hard that it was common for sailors to break their teeth on them.

The French settlers in the southern states of the USA were also fond of a few 'twice cookeds'. However, these biscuits were a sort of dumpling or cobbler, which were served with stews and gravy. When I say gravy I use the term in its loosest possible sense, as the 'gravy' most popular with biscuits is made from lumps of sausage, flour and sausage fat and is a glutinous, white, pasty-looking affair. Anyone who has spent time with a large family dog suffering from a weak stomach would have a powerful sense of déjà-vu if they asked for a plate of biscuits in the USA.

We can therefore at least sympathise with the imperative not to order the wrong sort of biscuits, which must have led to the adoption of the Dutch word over the French for the same thing. So, before we wade into the Americans for annoyingly calling their biscuits cookies, let's pause for a moment and blame the French instead. We might want to tick off the Dutch but I seriously doubt they would even notice.

that you have to be raised on them to like them. Outside of the US, I suspect it's sold mainly to Americans abroad or eccentrics, yet within its homeland it apparently enjoys sales of eleven billion a year (or four billion, it's hard to be sure).

The main ingredient in Oreos is our old friend sugar, which is used to fashion two dark cocoa biscuits decorated with the Oreo's logo. Sandwiched between is a layer of white stuff which is euphemistically called cream, but is probably best thought of as soft icing. Variations in the cream's depth and coatings of fudge also help shoehorn in extra quantities of sugar. In fact, the minty ones would probably put up a good fight against a slab of Kendal Mint Cake in terms of sheer carbohydrate loading potential.

Oreos seem to be supplied in cardboard boxes bearing eating instructions on their sides. To non-American eyes, the idea of putting instructions on how to eat a biscuit on the box might seem ridiculous. Little diagrams and captions tell you to disassemble your Oreo and then scrape out the white stuff, which, rather than discard, you're supposed to eat first. You are also advised to drink milk while doing this. Any Americans whom I've approached about this whole area become a bit prickly, saying it's all part of the ritual of the product, but it appears that the absurdity isn't entirely lost on them.

Still, it is a testament to the success of the Oreo and the strength of the brand that they are imitated around the world. Some time ago I got my hands on a pack of Hi-Ro from the Philippines, an Oreo-alike which a little misguidedly claimed to be of 'English Quality'.

Pocky

You are going to have to allow me a little leeway here, as we are about to visit a unique spot on the mighty biscuit Venn diagram: the triple union of biscuits, crackers and chocolate-covered biscuits. What do we find here? None other than the exceedingly odd Mikado, also known as Pocky, and not to be confused with Jacob's Mikado (see p.99).

Essentially a long, straight, salt-less pretzel 80 per cent dipped in chocolate, the Mikado is made by French biscuit manufacturer LU under licence from the Japanese snack firm Glico. LU make two varieties: the traditional plain chocolate one and a more recent milk chocolate version. In Japan one can find Pocky in strawberry, green tea, rainbow and even lime and watermelon flavours. I've been told that it offends Japanese sensibilities to touch the chocolate directly, hence the little lolly-stick uncovered bit. It also offends some people to hear Beatles songs being publicly murdered so Tokyo karaoke bars have bowls of Pocky on the tables to help ease the suffering. At least, I think that's why they're there.

As everybody no doubt knows, pretzels were invented by a seventh-century Italian monk, who was trying to come up with something that could be eaten during Lent. Given the restrictions on what could be consumed, he didn't have much to work with, namely flour, water and salt. Believe it or not, the first pretzels were soft, which is remarkable, given their ingredients: I would have thought they would have come out like bricks. It is believed that in order to remind the eater that Lent was a time of prayer, our baking monk formed the familiar pretzel shape as an echo of the folded arms of somebody at prayer. It's also thought that a possible derivation for 'pretzel' is the Latin word *pretiola* which means 'little reward'.

The kind monks gave pretzels to the poor, who, being poor, were grateful for them (though no doubt once the poor had sorted themselves out and got back on their feet, pretzels wouldn't be top of their shopping list). They were also given to children as a reward for reciting their prayers correctly. It appears that back in the seventh century children had a much lower threshold for bribery. The younger members of staff can't be persuaded to tidy their room for anything less than half a pack of Jaffa Cakes.

Eventually a baking accident led to pretzels becoming even harder, and with it smaller, I expect. This was seen as a bonus as they lasted longer and could be distributed to the poor with greater ease. By now the poor must have had quite a serious thirst on them, and were no doubt gasping for a pint or maybe a gin and tonic. Presumably at some point the Germans, who had a keen interest in drinking beer, must have noticed the crowds of poor beating a path from the monastery to their pubs after eating too many salty snacks. As a result, Germany took over the mantle of leading pretzel-making nation.

No doubt dry-roasted peanuts have a very similar story to tell.

 # Dunking

Dunking is probably as old as the first hot meal cooked by mankind. Whenever we look for the originators of stuff that is really old (but not cave man old) it always seems to be the ancient civilisations that grew up around the Tigris and Euphrates rivers in what is modern day Iraq, about 8,000 years ago. Sometimes it's the ancient Egyptians but that is so predictable. The ancient Sumerians don't seem to have so many TV documentaries as the rest so we'll give them a break and pretend they came up with it. Now of course I have no idea if this was actually the case but it sounds good doesn't it? Anyhow the Iraqis like a good pot of strong tea and a biscuit or cake if there is one going, so that is good circumstantial evidence.

Things probably didn't change much until the reign of Queen Victoria, who had just had a jam and cream sponge named after her. Not content with leaving her mark on the cake world, Victoria set her sights on the world of biscuits by inventing the Butter Osborne, after her much-loved holiday home on the Isle of Wight. And butter. Being a queen, and as it was her first go at biscuit invention, the results were a fairly grim, thick, chalky Rich Tea sort of biscuit. Insisting that her subjects eat at least one packet each on her birthday, it quickly became the fashion to dunk them, in order to successfully complete one's patriotic duty. No doubt the colonies decided they would take up dunking as well, just to be on the safe side.

Right, that's history rewritten. Let's take a look at some dunking techniques and issues.

How To Do It

To the casual observer, dunking is purely the act of submerging part of your biscuit in your tea, pulling it out and eating the wet bit. Anybody who has tried dunking or is a full-time dunking enthusiast will know that there is much, much more to it than that. Let's explore some of the things that can go wrong and strategies that you can use for successful dunking.

The Biscuit Is Too Big For The Cup

There are a few simple things that you can try here. First, simply try to find a larger cup. Second, choose smaller biscuits or those that lend themselves to dunking, such as finger-shaped or rectangular ones.

If you are hell bent on a particular combination of biscuit and cup despite the problems, then the first thing you can try is to break the biscuit in two, and dunking the two halves. This is of course a crude and unsightly technique but it's always there as an option. Its main drawbacks are the unnecessary creation of crumbs leading to 'bottom sludge' (see below), and the disfiguring of perfectly good biscuits. You could try taking a bite or two out of the biscuit, but this too is prone to creating crumbs. Try to minimise this with a mouth-hoovering action over the broken edges.

The experienced approach is called 'dunk nibble rotate'. This requires a fairly full cup or mug of tea to begin with, and it should be piping hot. In the case of round biscuits, even something as large as a Digestive will be able to dip a small portion of its edge into the cup to meet the hot tea. This creates a geometric line called a 'chord' whose endpoints lie on the circumference and whose perpendicular bisector passes through the centre of the circle. The angle theta subtended by joining the ends of the chord to the centre of the circle is crucial. The higher the value of theta, the quicker you'll be able to eat your biscuit. All fairly straightforward so far?

The dunked bit can then be nibbled off to create a slight corner. The biscuit should then be rotated so that a perpendicular line passes through the centre of the biscuit and the end of the chord. Either end will do: you don't have to be too scientific about it. This time much more of the biscuit will 'dip' into the hot tea and you'll be able to nibble off a bigger bit. Repeat the process until the biscuit is narrowed enough to fit into the mug when rotated through ninety degrees. Typically you should reach complete immersion potential in one to four dunk-nibble-rotate cycles. As the tea is absorbed or drunk the degree of difficulty increases until you reach the limit at which point the tea is too low to be reached by the biscuit edge. At this point simply revert back to the inferior crumb-prone techniques.

Don't worry if that sounded complex: it's really quite easy once you get used to it. It can also become quite an addictive pastime, with proponents getting a buzz by deliberately seeking out challenging large-diameter biscuits, although still avoiding small cups and mugs.

Bottom Sludge

The facets of dunking are interrelated so we have touched on sludge already. Bottom sludge is caused by crumbs falling to the bottom of the cup and creating a biscuity porridge. As you near the end of your tea, this sludge rushes down the edge of the cup or mug to meet you, like a small mud slide. While it is no doubt nutritious and maybe even tasty, being formed from biscuits and tea, the vast majority of people don't care for it, preferring to drink pure tea.

So what can be done to avoid sludge issues? The first and most obvious is to prevent the build-up of sludge in the first place, limiting the amount of biscuit crumbs. Here are some other simple tips:

 Always tap your biscuit a couple of times on the side of the biscuit tin to eliminate excess crumbs.

 Avoid broken or damaged biscuits for dunking, and if you do use them, dunk the unbroken side.

Avoid very crumbly biscuits or those with loosely attached frilly bits.

Breakage

It should always be remembered that dunking times will vary depending on tea temperature. Very hot tea will penetrate biscuits much faster than warm tea. Failure to compensate for tea temperature is one of the most common reasons for breakage, which is when the bottom of your biscuit fails to re-emerge from your tea, or drops off and falls back into your tea as you lift out the biscuit.

As a dunked biscuit absorbs tea, it begins to swell. Sugars in the biscuit begin to dissolve, fats melt, starch grains swell and unravel and the whole structure becomes soft and pliable. In addition, it becomes substantially heavier. If the tea has penetrated right to the biscuit's core, then there is a very high chance that breakage will occur. To lessen the risk, the biscuit should always be lifted vertically from the tea. Deviating from ninety degrees will cause the now heavier and flexible dunked portion to swing down to the vertical position like a plumb line, and this could cause a tear near to the dunking boundary, quickly leading to breakage.

When moving close to breakage, you should avoid rapid acceleration and deceleration. Overcoming the inertial mass of the damp biscuit can again lead to unscheduled breakage. This applies even if you are in a micro-gravity environment such as a plane in a parabolic freefall trajectory or lift that has become detached from its supporting cables. It's only going to make a bad situation worse if you drop half a soggy Rich Tea in your lap.

Differential Uptake

Sometimes biscuits can display a 'differential uptake' in tea across their structure. This is especially common in composite sandwich structures: outer surfaces may be baked harder than the inner, which may itself be porous. This can lead the tea to permeate at different rates across the biscuit. It's not really a problem; I just thought you might like to know, that's all. Once again, use a good hot cuppa and you'll be fine.

The Tim Tam Slam

The Tim Tam Slam goes by many names but the basic principle is very simple to grasp: it's simply a matter of using the biscuit as a straw. Due to the lightness of the biscuit, its airtight seal of chocolate, and its sprightly dimensions, the Tim Tam is eminently suited to this procedure. To perform the Tim Tam Slam, bite off diagonally opposed corners, pop one corner in your tea, the other in your mouth, and suck. The hot tea will off course wreak havoc on the little Antipodean biscuit's innards, leading to a complete and often catastrophic failure of structural integrity. For this reason you are advised to pop the whole thing into your mouth before it disintegrates. I would certainly recommend not doing this sort of thing in front of impressionable youngsters, unless you particularly enjoy frequent redecorating.

Although this might sound like a grubby old business, I have been told that in Australia the Tim Tam Slam is a perfectly acceptable activity whatever the social situation or occasion. As an alternative, the smaller Cadbury's Chocolate Finger is also very good for slamming.

A Little Bit
of Cake

 # Cake

Biscuits don't always have the attention of the teapot all to themselves. Often they have to share the table with small sandwiches and, more worryingly, with that other rival for our sweet-toothed affection, cake.

Cake has always taken itself much more seriously than the humble biscuit, which it considers merely as a supporting actor upon its own glittering stage. Biscuits are always ready for action, there at a moment's notice. Cake, on the other hand, likes to make a bit of an entrance by being nicely cut up and arranged on plates. It also likes to frequent exclusive little boutiques, called cake shops, where it can compare its fillings and diameters with other cakes. Cake loves being seen in the window, displaying its various toppings and fruits, both fresh and dried. Often such places have a little back room where cake, with the help of a pot of tea and maybe even a trolley, can entertain eager visitors.

Homemade cakes demand complete attention even when in the oven, and often take hours getting themselves made and decorated. They like to have nice things bought for them from the cake-making section in the supermarket, such as their own special bars of chocolate, which nobody else is allowed to touch.

Cake likes to trot out its part in history, like the time it got burnt by King Alfred. And who can forget its Gothic moment as Miss Havisham's decaying wedding cake in *Great Expectations*? It also insists that it gets invited to parties, which it often brings to a complete standstill, demanding that the music is turned off and the lights dimmed as it gets to do its little bit.

Cake manifests itself in a variety of ways, from the lowly tart to the grandest gateau, from a simple sticky bun to a candle-topped birthday cake. Plainly cake is a big subject and would like to have a whole book to itself, or a series of books, or a section in the library. However, we are going to look at just a few examples simply because they make me laugh.

Jaffa Cakes

The Eternal Debate

Throughout the course of human history there have been a few really big philosophical questions that have occupied the world's great minds. Does God exist? Is there a theory that can unify general relativity and quantum mechanics? However, 'Are Jaffa Cakes biscuits or cakes?' shouldn't be one of them, as they are plainly cakes. That's why they are called Jaffa *Cakes*, not Jaffa Biscuits. Simple. Let's move on. But this is a question that doesn't seem to want to go away. Who is the main culprit still insisting that the Jaffa Cake is a biscuit? None other than the civil service in the guise of the Inland Revenue. They have a vested interest, and would love the Jaffa Cake to be a biscuit. It all comes down to tax: when VAT was created, it was decided not to tax the staple things in life that we simply cannot do without, this fine book being one of them, of course. Cake is another. Biscuits, however, have to tread very carefully: it all comes down to where you put your chocolate. If it is discreetly hidden away in chunks or between two halves of biscuit, as in a chocolate Viennese finger, then the VAT man won't spot it. Slap it ostentatiously all over the top of your biscuit and he'll instantly tell you that your 'luxury' product is now liable for VAT.

ORANGES

When everything else is letting you down, there is one fruit above all others that you can rely on: the orange. Oranges have a special role in the universe by providing one of the key reference points in our perception of reality, and the bonus is that they grow on trees. Not only do oranges taste of orange, but they smell of orange. Their masterstroke, though, was to get a whole colour named after them. Not some dodgy made-up paint-chart colour like 'watermelon'. No, a proper colour that appears in the rainbow. To make sure that orange continues in its unassailable position it has even ensured that no new words have entered the English language that might properly rhyme with it. That's why there is no such thing as a 'boringe' or a 'morange', when plainly these are perfectly good words that deserve a chance.

This is the essential problem. If the Jaffa Cake were to be a biscuit, it would swiftly be taxed, where as a cake it gets away with it. Unsurprisingly, the Inland Revenue thought that the Jaffa Cake was really a biscuit while McVitie's knew it was a cake. The VAT Act of 1983 was a bit woolly about what constituted a cake, so in 1991 it fell to a tribunal to decide. First of all they thought about the sponge base, and accepted that it really was sponge cake, containing fat, sugar, eggs and flour, like sponge cake should. They worked out that it starts off moist and goes hard when stale, like a cake. Biscuits on the other hand start crisp and hard and go soft when stale. It was all looking rosy in the garden for McVitie's. But the tribunal then went on to consider that Jaffa Cakes were sold in packs of three up to twenty-four, and that they associated themselves with the biscuits in retail outlets. It looked like the tribunal was going to find in favour of the Inland Revenue, when McVitie's played their trump card in the form of a twelve inch-wide Jaffa Cake. The tribunal decided it needed a pot of tea to consider the evidence. One giant Jaffa Cake later, the tribunal concluded that, while the product had some of the characteristics of biscuits or confectionery, it had sufficient cake characteristics to be a cake for the purposes of zero-rating. (The Irish Inland Revenue, meanwhile, simply noted that 'moisture content >12% = cake'. Very sensible, though if they had made a scene maybe they too would have been able to have a crack at a few foot-wide Jaffa Cakes.)

Confusion still reigns, though, as people try to decide the nature of the 'smashing orangey bit in the middle'. Is it jelly or jam? In the UK we think of jelly as a colloidal state of the protein called gelatin. The smashing orangey bit, however, is set using pectin, a complex polysaccharide. Not only is this terrific news for vegetarians, but it means that we are dealing with jam. In fact, according to McVitie's, it's a form of industrial jam, which everybody knows is one level up from domestic jam, but not as impressive or possibly dangerous as military-strength jam.

There is one last important question about the Jaffa Cake that I feel remains as yet unanswered. With its domed sponge underside and its raised inner jammy bit, why doesn't anybody ever mention the fact that it looks like a little flying saucer? Is this so obvious that it doesn't require mentioning, or is it a giant conspiracy?

The combination of plain chocolate and tangy orange jam complement each other very well, but the Jaffa Cake also has some more exotic cousins, mostly in continental Europe. There is a dark cherry jam version with a white chocolate top, decorated with dark chocolate detailing, called Pims. They were last spotted in the UK in the 1980s. Today, in France, Pims are made with a moulded chocolate top and filled with orange, pear and lemon jam.

The Polish have many Jaffa Cake-alikes, with strawberry being used to good effect in their flavours. Reading Polish biscuit packets isn't much use if you don't speak Polish, though I found it very thought-provoking. For instance, the letter Z seems to enjoy immense popularity in Poland and is probably on a par with the letter N or maybe even F in this country. In fact, if it wasn't for the Polish I dare say we could have phased out the letter Z altogether a long time ago. That would have got the alphabet down to 25 letters that could be arranged in nice, neat five-by-five squares. Lovely. Most Polish people seem to have a few Zs in their names, thereby personally ensuring that the letter is still with us, and potentially they could help out by keeping the poor old Zebra company on the last page of any children's alphabet book.

All that is very well, but we all know deep down that the Jaffa Cake is really a biscuit. It lives beside the biscuits in my local supermarket, and when I tell people that my favourite biscuit is a Jaffa Cake they don't look at me in horror saying, 'But it can't be, it's a cake!' They just shrug, and even sometimes agree with me. I imagine the manufacturers also know it's really a biscuit but went to all the trouble of calling it a cake so that it would be zero-rated, therefore making it cheaper for us to buy.

I don't blame them for doing this. I blame our VAT system for being so complicated that such things become a problem. Hundreds of millions of pounds must be spent every year by the government employing people to decide if new products are cake or not, or if a biscuit has that little bit of extra chocolate that makes it a 'luxury'. My solution? Well, it's easy. The government should just admit that all biscuits are part of our staple diet. They would save a fortune and we could go back to admitting that the Jaffa Cake is really a biscuit. The biscuit manufacturers, meanwhile, could get back to the important task of making bigger, better, more chocolatey biscuits without fear of the tax man, who in turn could spend more time chasing proper tax-evading criminals. Simple.

Wedding Cake

Out of all the many cakes in the world, there is one more than any other which demands 'A'-list celebrity treatment: the prima donna of the baked goods world, the wedding cake. The ego of the wedding cake knows no bounds and often gets so completely overboard that it seems that the whole event has been contrived just so that it could come into existence.

THE HISTORY OF THE WEDDING CAKE

If wedding cake is feeling sorry for itself, it would do well to remember that the original wedding cakes, baked by the Romans, were simply thrown directly at the bride's head. Originally, handfuls of wheat were thrown, apparently as a sign of wealth, fertility and prosperity. Then, after a while, Roman bakers decided that it would be nice to make the wheat into little sweetened cakes; and the congregations simply started throwing these instead. It can't have been much fun being caught full in the face by what was essentially a crude Iron Age bun, and so it became good etiquette at least to crumble them up and sprinkle them over the bride's head. This was known as *confarreatio* or 'eating together', from which our word 'confetti' is derived.

In Britain, it became the custom to arrange the little cakes into enormous piles, the higher the better, to demonstrate that you obviously had loads of impressive wheat at your disposal. But these were forever falling over, which led a French chef – on a visit to London – to invent the tiered wedding cake.

Of course, the truth is that most wedding cakes are simply Christmas cake recipes that have been given the chance to play to a bigger crowd.

From the beginning, the wedding cake throws its weight around, demanding that it works with only the best. This is preferably a team of really experienced aunts plus their friend from over the road who does the icing. Special baking tins are commissioned and ovens have their diaries emptied to make way for some extra-long, six-hour cake jobs. It's quite usual in these early stages for a cake to hype up its forthcoming debut by circulating outrageous stories of its dried fruit consumption, coupled with its appetite for eggs. This is designed to intimidate the couple who will be taking to the stage alongside the cake when the big day comes. The electric mixer is pushed way beyond its theoretical design limits, as the mixing bowl becomes a culinary black hole, dragging in every last currant and glacé cherry in the neighbourhood. As the

mix grows ever larger, even exotic stuff like dried pineapple isn't safe. Even tea itself cannot escape, spiralling into the churning vortex.

It is at this formative stage in its career that the wedding cake, flushed no doubt with its successful removal of every last pack of chopped almonds from the local supermarket, reaches for the bottle. It all begins innocently enough: a couple of glasses of sherry, and maybe the odd tot of brandy. However, after a few days out of the oven, the cake starts complaining that it might be 'drying out a little' in its tin. The answer could be to splash a little more brandy over it. The cake likes this, and is soon demanding more and more brandy sessions on a regular basis. With only a few days left to go before it's due to be smeared with apricot jam and fitted with its marzipan under-layer, the cake embarrassingly sees off a whole bottle of Three Barrels brandy. For good measure, it then demands that it is doused with the last of a bottle of Johnny Walker Red Label. By now the cake has imbibed so much spirit that its underside has become distinctly mushy. It would be prudent not to smoke in its presence.

Any really impressive cake will need to be arranged in tiers, although how it is planning on remaining upright after all that booze is anybody's guess. Luckily, the experienced team of aunts swings into action and, having dealt with many a dipsomaniac cake in the past, know that a cake board and a good strong supporting coat of royal icing will do the trick. Finally, after donning its sugar flowers and ribbons, the wedding cake is ready for its big day.

To meet its public properly, the wedding cake gets its own table to sit on. The lucky bride and groom have their picture taken with it. Eventually the cake's big moment arrives and a special silver knife is called for, which has no other purpose than the glorious ceremonial doing-in of cakes. The happy couple pretends at some length to cut the cake with the ceremonial silver cake knife. The cake breathes a palpable sigh of relief as these amateurs are quickly led away and it is handed over to a dedicated team of skilled cake-cutters. Of course, the cutters have to deal with the cake's all-too-obvious drink problem, which can lead to lumps of it falling to pieces under the slightest pressure.

The wedding cake now faces its first big challenge: will anybody actually like it? This isn't going to be an easy gig as the audience has already eaten their fill of starter, main course and dessert. In addition, quite a few are drunk and there are also those who don't like marzipan, others who don't like icing and even those who admit to not even liking cake itself, any cake. There follows the probing and personal questions that are fielded by the cake's crack team of aunts. Just what is in it? Straight away, those with nut, wheat, dairy and egg allergies rule themselves out. In fact, anyone who is allergic to, or in some way has a problem with, any given substance should stay well clear of any wedding cake, as no doubt it contains at least four ounces of it. Still, the cake makes the best of it, aided by some very helpful pots of tea and even some coffee. Before long the compliments start to flow, and the cake can be proud that it is 'lovely and moist' (there is apparently nothing worse than a 'dry' cake). Though how many of the wedding party have been rendered unfit for driving by a portion of cake is another matter.

If anybody thought they could sneak off without a piece of cake then they didn't reckon on its final wish, that it be carved up and distributed to all and sundry wrapped in serviettes. The bitter truth, however, is that most of these pieces of cake are given to children who, after picking off the icing, abandon the rest of the alcohol-pickled remains. These are then unceremoniously consigned to the pedal bin, still conveniently shrouded in their serviette.

I would just like to add that Nicey and I were very sneaky and only gave the aunties (i.e., my mother) and the 'friend over the road' (i.e., Norma from next door) six weeks' notice of our impending wedding. Nonetheless, we had a wonderful wedding cake that managed to hold its own, despite being ignored for quite some time while we all had a barbecue in our back garden.

Lovely.

Fairy Cakes

A few years ago Wifey and I were in France doing a spot of wine tasting with a view to buying a few cases of 'deep strike' wine to bring back to Blighty. Flushed with the success of selling us two cases of the Cuvée St George, the chap at the cave (though this one was in fact a large shed) insisted that we try the local speciality wine, called 'Gris'. This was a pale pink, thin, stalky affair. I think our stifled grimaces told the chap that he needed to hit the hard sell, so he ventured that (literally excuse my French), '*C'est bien avec les petits gateaux dans l'apres-midi.*' For any of you whose French is even worse than mine, he was advocating drinking it in the afternoon while eating small cakes.

It's funny how so such a small phrase can convey such big cultural differences. I don't know what sort of country the French are running over there, but sitting around drinking wine and eating cakes all afternoon isn't going to get the bills paid. Mind you, this could explain why the rural French lunch hour seems to extend from midday on the dot to about 3 p.m. It takes an hour or two to sleep off all that cake and booze.

So, I've managed to mention small cakes there, but not fairy cakes specifically, only now I have. For many people, the fairy cake is 'the' small cake. For some, it's the rock cake; and for others, if it doesn't have cream in it then it's not even worth talking about. Despite its small size, the fairy

GLACÉ CHERRIES

There is one very simple way to make a small cake happy, and that is to put a glacé cherry on top of it, or even just half a glacé cherry. A properly specified slice of Genoa fruit cake should ideally have at least two cross-sectional glacé cherries clearly visible, and any proper full-spectrum fruit cake needs its helping of glacé cherries.

But just what are glacé cherries and where do they come from? Surprisingly, glacé cherries are actually made using fairly conventional cherries that grow on trees. This is startling stuff because, apart from their size, glacé cherries are almost nothing like their straight-off-the-tree counterparts. So what is this dramatic transformational process that can render a normally opaque cherry into a semi-transparent entity, and is it called 'glacé-ing'? The sad truth is it's not called 'glacé-ing', but 'candying', which is a dangerously transatlantic type of word. A firm-fleshed white cherry, after being washed with a yeast-killing solution containing E220 (sulphur dioxide), is bathed in increasingly concentrated syrup solutions. Then some E127 (erythrosine) or maybe E120 (see 'Pink Icing' on p.150), and some E202 (potassium sorbate) are added to colour it red and to stop it going off. A great deal of glacé cherries are produced in France, but, not really having much use for them, the French send most of them to Britain.

I'm surprised that there hasn't been a super-villain who has used glacé-ing in some form of world domination, or at the very least a big gun capable of glacé-ing things. I wonder what glacéd dogs, cars or postboxes would be like, and if they would be suitable for baking.

cake is really a party animal and doesn't mind mixing it with the big boys, such as birthday cakes, even if they are decked out in ribbons with rock and roll flames on their tops. The fairy cake's secret is to travel around by the plateload, which can be quite impressive. If birthday cakes don't want to risk being upstaged by their warm-up act they should up the ante by getting some dry ice, lightning flashes and a laser show.

The exact specification of a fairy cake seems to be a little vague, but what is universally agreed upon is that it's a small sponge cake baked in its own paper case. As the cake bakes, a small domed peak is formed. Some designs, which probably gave rise to the name, call for this peak to be sliced off, cut in two and placed back on top, stuck down with some form of butter-cream or icing. This gives the impression of two small wings. However, I always thought that they were called angel or butterfly cakes. Most fairy cakes simply make do with a coating of water icing, and a glacé cherry half or a couple of pieces of angelica.

Packet Cakes

Not all cakes give themselves such airs and graces as the likes of the celebration wedding, birthday and Christmas cakes. Some cakes are quite humble and approachable: they still like being sliced up and put on a plate, but they are happy enough to turn up at Sunday tea-time, or even on a picnic. These packet cakes don't want to make a big fuss and will cheerfully make do with a bit of a wrapper, and at the most a thin sheet of cardboard folded into three. They also don't mind a bit of light, good-natured stacking when sitting on the shelves.

Pink icing is intrinsically more fun than white icing, as it is obviously frivolous compared to white icing's implied purity and slightly prim appearance. Being halfway to sinful red, pink is therefore moderately wanton and semi-hedonistic. Any cake looking for a good time is going to pop on its pink icing and red cherry.

A couple of drops of cochineal is all that is needed to make a bowl of pink icing, so a tiny bottle gives years of service. I think most people know that the red food colour cochineal (E120) is made from crushed insects, but they choose to push that to the back of their minds, as it's not too pleasant. That's not going to stop me from going on about it at some length though.

The first and most obvious question is why on earth are these little insects so keen on being filled with bright red dye? Second, and equally obviously, what are the squished insides of beetles doing in my cake?

Actually, they're not beetles but scale insects, which are a little like aphids inasmuch as they live by plunging their proboscis into a plant and letting the sap flow through them, taking what they need. In the case of *Dactylopius coccus*, or the cochineal scale, it is a type of prickly pear cactus. The insect secretes a waxy coat, and any excess sap simply passes out of the back. This is where the red pigment carminic acid comes in: it is an excellent ant-repellent. This comes in handy when some of the nastier ants aren't just interested in your excess sap, but want a main course of scale insect.

It was the Aztecs who first cultivated the cactus and the insects to provide a source of textile dye. When the Spanish arrived, they considered the dye the second most valuable commodity after gold. Two and a half centuries later, the Spanish monopoly on cochineal production was broken when a French naturalist smuggled some cactus pads from Haiti. Today, Peru and the Canary Islands are the main producers. The dye is now used in everything from sausages to lipstick.

Ginger Cake

Has there ever been a cake that likes its packet as much as the Ginger cake? It would rather you tore its bottom and sides off than part it from its extra-large baking case. Just to show how serious it is about remaining wedded to its case, ginger cake saves its stickiest and tastiest bits for attaching to the wrapper. This can often mean that the wrapper is the best bit of a ginger cake, a bit like the crackling is the best bit of roast pork. Scraping it off the wrapper requires a straight knife, not too sharp and not too blunt. Having finally separated the outside from the wrapper it may be formed back into a lump, though this has a tendency to over-compress it, so it's best eaten with the fingers from small heaps in the wrapper.

Battenberg

Battenberg cake steals the show every time. Its nearest rival technically in the two-coloured-sponge arena is marble cake, but this knows better than to go up against the barking mad Battenberg. But where is Battenberg and why are its cakes so pink and yellow, and smell of almonds?

Yet again, the crowned heads of Europe are involved. This time it's the Germans, and if you've just quipped that I must mean the British royal family you'd be right. The German town of Battenberg has given its name to a fair proportion of Europe's royalty, our own included. When Austrian-born Prince Louis of Battenberg married Princess Victoria of Hesse-Darmstadt, granddaughter of Queen Victoria, in 1884, everybody was so pleased that the new Battenberg cake was invented. In 1917, due

to World War One Prince Louis relinquished his German titles and took the Anglicised surname Mountbatten.

As everybody knows, a Battenberg consists of two square strips of pink sponge and two of yellow, arranged to form a larger square check. The whole lot is wrapped in a sheet of marzipan and stuck together via that all-purpose cake glue, apricot jam. Why this was felt to be evocative of German royalty I don't know. Perhaps they smell strongly of almonds. Nevertheless, the Battenberg is a splendid cake, and once you become acclimatised to it you will find it hard to resist.

I would be more than a little tempted to pick the Battenberg as my cake of choice in a first-contact-with-aliens situation. It's so cheerful, no matter what wavelengths of light your visual receptors are attuned to. Of course, there is always the possibility in common with some earthlings that they might find marzipan to be toxic, which is fair enough. Although, if they are going to jaunt around the universe, dropping in on people at random, then they have to expect that sort of thing. If they have any manners they'll eat it politely, say what they've come to say, then run back to their spaceship to keel over while searching for an antidote.

And a Sit Down

 # Sitting Down

It goes without saying that for a nice cup of tea you need a sit down. Just the same, we always take the belt and braces approach and say, 'A nice cup of tea and a sit down', as this leaves no room for error.

It is often said of people who are engaged in sitting down that they are doing 'nothing': for example, 'Why are you sitting down doing nothing?' They're not doing 'nothing', of course. For a start they are breathing, using their intercostal rib musculature and diaphragm. Their liver is doing any number of the five hundred different things that it is responsible for. The digestive system is busily at work on their breakfast which is contributing to the eleven and a half litres of stuff that flows through it each day. Their heart is pumping up to five litres of blood around the body at any one time, expending in one hour enough energy to raise a one-ton weight by a yard. Their body is renewing its very cellular structure at the phenomenal rate of fifty thousand cells a second. One hundred billion neurons and sixty trillion synapses in their brain are helping them sit there and think about it all, or what is for dinner.

No wonder they'll be needing a nice cup of tea and a biscuit.

When we want to stretch somebody to the limits of human coordination, we ask them to rub their tummy with one hand and pat their head with the other, all while standing up. For most people this simply exceeds their physical limits, even when sober. This is why very few activities require you to do it. The early pioneers of the motor car, for example, avoided control systems that required you to rub your tummy and pat your head simultaneously, settling instead on a steering wheel and some pedals and levers. Interestingly, they still thought you should be sitting down to work all of that. In fact, right across the whole gamut of man–machine interaction we see the sit down as integral, from the operation of sewing machines and military attack helicopters to watching TV and manoeuvring those big lawn-mowers that you can sit on.

Given the fine level of control needed to correctly make and pour tea, to properly unwrap and eat a Club biscuit or to successfully dunk a Digestive, it really isn't tenable that this should be attempted while standing up. Not that we are advocating a sedentary lifestyle. We think people should all get out of the house and go for nice walks and bike rides, that sort of thing. As well as being good for you, you can burn off enough calories to justify a pot of tea and some biscuits and a nice sit down when you get back in.

The Folly of Not Sitting Down

The stand-up buffet is all the evidence required for any evolved society to condemn the practice of standing around trying to relax while eating and drinking. There are simply too many verbs here for anybody to be truly at ease: standing, talking, eating and drinking. Let's not forget spilling, balancing, dropping and swearing as some of the other doing words. On top of that you are probably expected to be talking, listening, mingling and on occasion even clapping. All of this while juggling a glass of red wine, a plate, a fork, a napkin and a selection of delightful morsels, most of which seem to be designed either to pour onto the floor or roll off your plate with all the ease of a handful of steel ball-bearings.

Sometimes hot food is served at a buffet which is bathed in pungent and powerfully staining sauces. Not only can this stuff scald you but it will leave indelible orange stains on all natural and man-made fibres. It's also effective on tricky, normally hard-to-stain surfaces such as glazed ceramics, glass, polytetrafluoroethane (Teflon), stainless steel and fingers. Any that is left over can be used in those briefcases that spray coloured stuff all over their contents when they are stolen, or to brand cattle. If they can't run to a hot buffet then the caterers will make sure that everybody gets a plentiful helping of pickled beetroot, piccalilli or something apparently preserved in ink.

Modern buffets have cutting-edge crockery and accessories intended to ease your predicament. However, strange plates with recesses or clip-on plastic devices designed to hold your wine glass just confer upon you the capability to spill your food and drink simultaneously.

Why is this inflicted upon us? As with most things we don't like, we are usually told that it is good for us. Apparently it is so that we can mingle with one another. I don't know about other nations but the British don't like to mingle; it's not something we are comfortable with. Huddle, yes; mingle, no. Most British people have mastered from an early age the skill of appearing to be approachable while avoiding all eye contact with other people. Unless they are carrying a tray of drinks.

Mingling requires talking to complete strangers, which limits the topics of conversation. Asking about them can be seen as being nosy, while talking about yourself can be seen as blowing one's own trumpet. So this whole area of interaction is best avoided. Subjects such as how nasty the wine is, how long the queue for the food was, why are there no chairs and what exactly is that stuff which is preserved in ink are all good. These, though, are quickly exhausted and long, uncomfortable silences will ensue during which people pretend to be more interested in their buffet lunch than they really are.

By far the best ice-breaker at these events is some form of minor disaster. If you are organising such a gathering, maybe you can arrange for the sprinkler system to be turned on for forty-five seconds. Or you may like to purchase, at very little cost, some form of old motor vehicle and burn it out in the car park near to where people will be entering the building. Both of these diversions will give people ample and sociably acceptable reasons to talk to one another. Mother Nature may even give you a hand and arrange some form of freak meteorological event like a blizzard, torrential rain, or a pleasantly warm spring day.

Often we are told, should we be stroppy enough to enquire, that sitting down is too expensive, so much so that the only practical course of action is to stand. Typically at such cut-price stand-up affairs, we are taunted by a huge pile of stacked chairs at one end of the function room, or in an adjoining room, often with tables too. People are frequently tempted to get some of the prohibited chairs and snatch some illicit sit downs. They probably would if it weren't for the fact that their hands were full of glasses, plates, forks and so on.

Sometimes people are driven to perching on stairs, doorsteps, window sills or even serving tables, risking certain chastisement from the caterers. This is all fairly demeaning and most will resist the temptation, preferring to suffer along with the crowd, their dignity intact. People sometimes complain, but only to one another, so it doesn't really get them very far. Most simply put up with it, afraid that they will be accused of not being sophisticated enough to cope with the ordeal of a stand-up buffet, or stigmatised as a non-mingler.

All proceeds to plan right until the point when tea, biscuits and cakes are served. This is enough to tip most people over the edge, and they will seek out a sit down at all costs. While they were happy to spill red wine and coleslaw down their suits and over their shoes in the feigned pursuit of chit-chat, tea is a much more serious business. To be fair, it's usually cake that causes the problems. Biscuits don't mind perching on the saucer, even though the chocolate-covered ones might melt against the side of the hot cup. Cake, being cake, demands its own little plate, and most people, having been born with a strict limit of two hands, are unable to cope. Some people will just up and leave, maybe taking their cake and tea with them. They will wander forlornly around the entire establishment and venture into the grounds looking for a place to sit down. They could turn up virtually anywhere: cupboards, lavatories, even wandering around in the street.

In such crisis situations, unlikely bands of people will gather, all united by a common struggle. This is the classic plot line for disaster movies such as *The Poseidon Adventure*, *Earthquake*, *Daylight* and *The Little Mermaid*. Groups of displaced people will trail around together, holding open doors with elbows for the other cup and saucer and cake plate-laden attendees, all trying to find a decent sit down. It may take weeks for the caterers to find all of the cups and saucers, some of which may be up to a quarter of a mile away from the original buffet lunch.

Sit Down Technique

The main aim when sitting down with a cup of tea is to relax. Any distractions or issues that may interfere with this must be ruthlessly eliminated.

The first requirement is that you are safely and comfortably seated. A chair or settee is almost always the best choice for a sit down as they have been designed specifically for that purpose. Always try to choose one that isn't clapped out with missing springs, incorrectly plumped cushions or bits of wire or cane that jab into your important sitting down areas. Make sure it's situated on level ground and not likely to tip over. If your seat is some form of folding or camping chair, ensure that it has been correctly erected. If you can't guarantee this then you may as well video your sit down, just in case you can sell it to one of those TV programmes that feature half an hour of people falling over. Actually, if you are going to all that trouble, you might want to locate your chair in a paddling pool while cuddling a cat against its will, and get a friend to ride their motorbike into you.

If chairs aren't available and you are forced to perch on the edge of a low wall or fence then always check for structural integrity. There is nothing less relaxing than having your lower body unexpectedly buried in rubble or splintered planks disappearing up the back of your jumper. Moisture is also an issue, especially on moss-covered walls, and unless you take precautions such as sitting on a waterproof coat or plastic bag, not only will the experience be unpleasant but those following you may question your ability to control your bladder functions.

Finally, you may be forced to consider a low step or even the ground itself. Try to ensure that you can comfortably get up again once the sitting down has come to an end. If this doesn't seem likely then try to establish an escape route by which you can crawl off on your hands and knees until a suitable standing-up location is reached. When sitting on the floor, be prepared for other people to tread on you, walk backwards over you and just generally treat you as a second-class citizen. Psychologists may put this down to submissive body language due to your prostrate position, but really it's because other people can't see you down there.

Your next most pressing issue is where to set down your tea and biscuits, and once again stability plays a major role, as does convenience. Some people will often trade one off against the other, choosing the arm of a chair despite its being too narrow or rounded to support their sundry cups and plates safely. Others will choose a solid nearby table or shelf, which, although stable, requires that they lean wildly out of their seat, thereby compromising the first requirement of seat stability. Worse still is having to stand up slightly to reach your cup, thus briefly terminating the sit down state itself. Armchairs with nice big wide flat arms are a boon to anybody seeking a self-contained sit down. My Aunty Dot used to have a three-piece suite in black vinyl which had big flat wooden fingernail things on the ends of the arms like built-in coasters. But this was Essex in the 1970s. Perhaps Western civilisation has only ever surpassed this degree of sit down convenience with Jimmy Savile's *Jim'll Fix It* chair, though this seemed mainly full of cigars delivered through flaps by bits of old coat-hangers. It only did this very rarely, no doubt due to the high probability that it could have had somebody's eye out.

Often the best option is a small table, perhaps from a nest of tables, that can be situated immediately adjacent to your seat. In some households, the competition for these may be fierce and when combined with issues such as line of sight to TV screens can create certain optimal chairs. Such prized seats are typically claimed by either the alpha male or the cat, whichever has the higher social ranking.

24 Moving Vehicles

The wheel is often cited as the most significant invention in human history (or fire or electricity or boats or something). Whatever it was, whenever we come up with some new form of transport, it's only a matter of time before we try to work out some way of drinking tea in or on it. Be it an ocean liner or a jumbo jet, it seems that we enjoy rising above the tawdry details of the engines and drive shafts propelling us to our destinations by having a nice cup of tea and a sit down. Often we'll read a book or the paper while we're at it. In fact, you might be sitting on a train or plane reading this and thinking about having a cup of tea. Perhaps somebody else somewhere is thinking about a man who is writing a book about somebody else on a train thinking about tea. Perhaps it's that bloke over there by the window. Give him a bit of a look; he'll soon stop it.

Trains

Einstein used to think about trains a lot. They used to crop up all the time in his 'thought experiments'. Einstein would try to deduce what would be observed by various people should they be aboard trains travelling at, or near to, the speed of light. Mainly, it would be lots of weird stuff involving people on the train having a different perception of time passing to that experienced by those in the station. Nothing too revolutionary there, then. But what would happen to their tea at such colossal speeds? I would be surprised if they didn't spill it, much like myself on the 8.15 King's Cross train, which I take from time to time. In fact, Einstein would have probably have needed to imagine a few serviettes in there as well, and some of those little three-packs of Custard Creams would be nice while he's at it.

Even with the new electrified line to London, there are still enough jolts and lurches as the train makes its progress that anybody holding tea has to enter an almost trance-like state if they are to avoid throwing it all over themselves. Much like some form of Eastern martial art, tea drinkers must develop keen senses and agile yet graceful movements. Sensing the motion of the train below, they must react quickly yet smoothly to the rocking and swaying. The drinker must become at one with the cup *and* the train, and in doing so create harmony between the two. Of course, knowing in advance when it's going to cross a set of points is also an advantage.

Grand masters of tea drinking on trains will remove the plastic lid from their cup as soon as their tea has brewed. Novices or habitually rigid people tend just to remove it for sips, which they take typically when the train chooses to cross some points. Drinking tea on trains always turns my mind to shaving with an old-fashioned cut-throat razor while surfing. I don't know if Einstein used to think about that. Probably not.

Coaches

As a young man I used to travel from one side of the country to the other by coach, Norwich to Wales, in a mere nine and a half hours, with an hour and a half stopover in Victoria Coach Station, fending off the pigeons with a rolled-up copy of the *New Scientist*. Coach travel, even 'luxury' coach travel, seems like something that human rights protesters might want to take a closed look at. Should you happen to be one of those unlucky people whose femurs are longer than the spacing between the coach seats, then conventional sit downs are ruled out. In order to fit into such a confined space, it becomes necessary to fold into three, with the legs drawn up so your knees are level with your teeth. Smashing your face into your knees as the coach slows down or accelerates is all part of the rhythm and majesty of coach travel.

Deploying your seat-back tray in readiness for a warmish drink is fairly tricky, as it is directly behind your knees. Moving your knees to one side means that you'll probably bash them against the knees of the person next to you. Mind you, by now your close proximity to one another will mean that you've already swapped your entire complement of bodily microbial flora, and have learnt to breathe in as they breathe out to keep the air pressure equalised, and stop your ears popping. In fact, after three hours you'll have exchanged germs with the entire bus, all of which will be fighting it out with your beleaguered immune system to see which is going to make you ill for the next week and a half.

If you are able to get your hand physically into your pocket to rescue enough money then you can purchase your paper cup of instant tea. Experienced coach travellers, who have normally already bagged the window seats, will have readied their refreshments money before getting on. You can spot these people as they may be seen clenching a couple of pound coins between their teeth, and hoping that their knees don't propel them down their throat.

Under normal circumstances you wouldn't contemplate drinking coach tea. However, you will be in a highly suggestive frame of mind. This will have been brought on by ninety minutes of a loud yet incomprehensible soundtrack for a video which is being displayed on a TV screen the size of a beer mat forty feet away. This is the type of thing the CIA used to subject South American dictators to when they had been naughty or were trying to hide in their palace compounds. After an hour and a half of it, struggling to work out if the movie is set in space, under the sea or maybe in the Wild West, you'll happily take anything that is offered to you as you strive to keep your higher brain functions from shutting down permanently.

Finally, as the coach draws near to its destination it will often toy with its weary and disorientated passengers by taking a convoluted round-the-houses approach, often passing the same point several times, and cheerfully plunging itself into unnecessary queues of traffic. Taking it out on the driver is ill-advised, as his state of mind is questionable, with him being a chain-smoker who has just gone three and a half hours without a cigarette.

When the passengers eventually disembark their brain deprogramming is complete. If you were looking to build an army of brainwashed clones to wreak havoc on an unsuspecting world then it might be an idea to hang around Victoria Coach Station and scoop up people as the get off the coach from Norwich. As a bonus, they won't be too choosy about their tea either.

Planes

Airliners are essentially large flying coaches, capable of speeds of 500 miles an hour at heights of 37,000 feet above the earth's surface. The safety talk before take-off is designed to remind you of this, and of what will happen should things go wrong. Of course, most people have listened to the safety talk countless times and don't pay any attention. In order to keep people focused on the details of the talk many stewardesses have taken to wearing bizarre and improbable make-up as a shock tactic. Drawing eyebrows in odd places and painting on mouths which are much larger than normal can make them the centre of attention. However, this often backfires as you try to imagine what their face really looks like under all that stuff, rather than listening to where all the doors and yellow inflatable things are. Everything else about the flight, including the tea, is designed to divert your attention from the fact that you are on a plane.

One of the cleverest techniques at the disposal of airlines for keeping passengers absorbed in concentration is food miniaturisation. This achieves two things. First, your seat, although being merely a glorified coach seat, appears much bigger as your brain struggles to make sense of the miniature bread roll now in your possession. Looking just like a normal bread roll, this chap has been scaled down to a mere one-fifth of its normal size. The same applies to chops, chickens, peas and apple pie with custard. All painstakingly reduced in size, using advanced jet-age catering technology.

Their second cunning trick is to supply a plastic sachet which contains hundreds of smaller sachets, rather like the catering equivalent of a cluster bomb. Cataloguing and finding somewhere to put all of the little

Homeostasis is our body's ability to keep a constant internal environment in terms of chemical balance and temperature. No matter if we are in a rainforest, on the Arctic tundra or somewhere in Bedfordshire sitting on our behinds watching the telly, our body maintains a core temperature of thirty-seven degrees Celsius. But before we get too cocky and start slapping one another on the back for being miracles of biological engineering, let's consider how useless we are unless we've recently had a decent cup of tea.

Some activities deplete our tea reserves faster than others, and by studying exactly which ones are most draining, we can better prepare for the possibility of chronic tea loss. Here is a list of the main culprits:

- Shopping
- Working
- Any form of DIY
- Sitting down
- Swimming
- Driving to the shops
- Mending things
- Housework
- Thinking about previous cups of tea
- Going upstairs then coming back down again
- Visiting other people
- Reading the paper
- Breakfast
- Watching other people do DIY on telly
- Walking to the shops
- Being outside
- Talking to pets in comedy voices
- Being on holiday
- Vacuuming the car
- Days beginning with the letter S
- Having people visit you

In fact, most things I could think deplete our tea reserves. Among the few things that don't increase the need to drink tea, however, are tea advertisements. Perhaps it is because our favourite brand of tea is drunk by plasticine birds. The sight of birds drinking tea just doesn't trigger the brain's tea response. I'm not really sure why tea needs to advertised at all. It's a bit like running adverts to encourage us to breathe more.

sachets that spill out when it is opened keeps you occupied for ten min-utes. Among it you'll find your knife, fork, spoon, teaspoon, coffee whitener, sugar, sweetener, toothpick, milk pot, salt, pepper, serviette, lemon-scented clean-up wipe, some more salt and pepper and maybe a little thing containing jam. Some people who are still used to travelling by coach are dazzled by such booty, and despite having no need for most of it now, or indeed later, insist on stuffing the extra salt and peppers, sweet-ener, toothpick and coffee whitener into their flight bags. They then carry most of this around with them for the next fortnight looking for an oppor-tunity to use it. Perhaps the salt could be utilised to despatch a small slug or clear a few square centimetres of path of snow and ice. The pepper could be used to divert a medium-sized cat from one small potted plant. The coffee whitener and sweetener, however, are next to useless unless you want to tamper with somebody's tea maliciously.

When the tea finally makes its appearance, it does so against its will, having been made with water that has 'boiled' at a much lower temper-ature than 100 degrees due to the cabin pressure. It also takes an eternity working its way down the rows of passengers only to run out at the chap in front of you. This ensures you get an extra-weak cup out of the new pot that turns up ten minutes later.

By the way, any attempt to take the miniature bread rolls with you when disembarking will meet with failure, as they can survive only in the rarefied environment of an airliner. Taking them into the everyday mortal world will cause them to shrivel up, like alpine flowers plucked from a high mountain or some other lovely metaphor to do with fairies. It's kinder to leave the bread rolls, even the unpleasant wholemeal ones, in their natural environment.

⟨25⟩ Tea in Public

Some people seem to need to drink cup after cup of tea in an endless chain just to remain functional. For such people, simple undertakings such as a visit to the shops are fraught with the spectre of ten minutes without a cup of tea. Often they will imbibe whole pots of the stuff before venturing outside in a bid to load their entire system with tea. Of course, there is always the prospect of using some artificial aid to unscheduled tea drinking such as a thermos flask, or one of those little element things that plug into a car cigarette lighter for boiling up water. But, for most, resorting to such things is an all too graphic way of admitting they have a problem. They would rather battle on, grabbing a cup of tea whenever and wherever they can.

By far the most socially acceptable way of obtaining tea in public is to visit some form of café, tea shop or in-store restaurant. Here you can enjoy tea with other tea drinkers in a supportive environment. Clever use of tables and chairs creates areas where you can sit down, and a range of cakes, pastries and till-side biscuits can help to make tea drinking more of a social event and less of a biological imperative.

If you think this is something that you might like to try, or if you are keen to meet other people who drink tea openly in public, then there are a few things you should know. The first and most obvious is price. Most tea shops are family affairs run by people who also share an interest in tea and sit downs, and in general you'll be well treated. However, at larger concerns, such as in-store cafés, you might find the less welcoming face of the tea business. Forced to wear ill-fitting and unfashionable uniforms, many youngsters find themselves serving tea for the minimum wage. As a tea drinker you don't have too much to worry about as it's quite difficult to mess up pouring hot water into a pot, and in general they won't try to force you to buy curled up lasagne, peas and chips. They might, however, simply depress you a little with their miserable conduct. They may also desert their posts, leaving you to stand there like a lemon at the till, with a tray bearing no more than a couple of teaspoons and a packet of shortbread fingers.

If you find anyone wanting to charge you more than two British pounds for tea then you should move on to another establishment. When all is said and done tea is a few dried leaves, a bit of hot water and a dash of milk. In fact, anything over eighty pence and you should begin to carp on about it being a disgrace. Failure to do so may result in your being mistaken for a tourist.

Second, you need to check on quantities. It's no good paying, say, £1.50 for an individual pot of tea only to find that it holds just a single cupful. There really is very little point in making teapots so small. Again, unless you want to look like a tourist, demand a second pot of boiling water, to top it up with. It's worth noting that most individual pots will actually pour more of your tea onto the table than into your cup, especially the little stainless-steel ones, so you really can't afford to start off with short measures. Also, watch out for shallow cups or those with overly thick sides, or, worse still, both. These are for small cups of coffee, not for big cups of tea.

Beware of those establishments that constantly froth up jugs of milk using the steam wand from an espresso machine (unless you actually enjoy the sound of a jet fighter with its afterburners on reheat, just a few metres from the back of your head). You may very, very occasionally have your tea made with hot milk left over from the deafening coffee palaver, either by accident or design. This is morally and technically wrong, and you are within your rights to cause an unpleasant scene should you choose to do so.

Milk is always going to be an issue. Ideally you will be given a small jug of chilled, pasteurised milk. You might be given access to a shared jug of milk, which is fine if you are not in a teapot scenario. Occasionally you'll need to grapple with those little plastic pots of milk. Avoid the brown ones: yet again they are for coffee. Also try to avoid dual-purpose for 'coffee and tea' pots, as these tend to be something other than milk. That's fine for coffee but not really for tea which can come out a bit greasy. If you don't actually get to see the milk but in some way have ready-whitened tea dispensed straight into your cup then leave immediately, and request that the local constabulary cordon off the area.

Another thing to look for is a supply of proper teaspoons. Metal teaspoons are a good indicator that you can expect something that at least approximates to tea. Plastic teaspoons are well meaning but indicate that the staff may not take the business of tea quite as seriously as you do. Anywhere that provides those long pointy stirring things will likely as not have a very cavalier attitude to tea and sit downs, and will be more comfortable serving you a large cardboard bucket of cola-flavoured ice. If you are unsure which end of the stirring thing is for holding and which end is for stirring, don't worry. It doesn't matter. Besides, this is the least of your problems: you should be more concerned about possible puncture wounds should you trip and fall on top of it while carrying a scalding-hot paper cup of tea back to your uncomfortably small plastic seat.

The quality of the tea is something that you might care to be concerned with, and often the brand of tea will be displayed or will be obvious from the tea bag supplied. If you are somewhere that serves tea from behind the counter out of a huge teapot then you should just drink it down with gusto, whatever it is like. Not only is it probably very strong and a bit stewed but it's no doubt going to be very effective. Finding out what sort of tea is actually in there is purely academic. If they also happen to sell bacon sandwiches then you should have one of those too. Ideally, I would like to see some form of standard sign outside these establishments saying, 'We serve tea out of an enormous teapot. Really, it's huge.'

The next step up is obviously the tea urn, to which the above also applies. Sometimes you will be given all sorts of fancy tea bags to choose from, which is all well and good, but such opulence usually comes at a price. The rule of thumb is for every extra variety of tea they recite, expect to add another ten pence to the price of a cuppa. At such an establishment you should always take the fight to them and ask for a blend of tea that they don't stock before grudgingly accepting one which they do. This will create a stabilising air of mutual pomposity in which to carry out your tea-purchasing transaction.

Vending Machines

The vending machine is the beverage equivalent of a fruit machine. If you are lucky, you'll get something you can drink delivered into your cup. If you are unlucky, you'll get something unknown poured over the back of your hand. Anybody who has had to depend on a vending machine for their tea will be carrying around the emotional and sometimes physical scars of experience. Let's face it, anything that produces tea, coffee, vegetable soup and lime squash while making a noise like a bin lorry compacting rubbish should be viewed with deep suspicion.

Many vending machines have their own idiosyncratic twists. The refusal to dispense drinks into anything but their own flimsy plastic cups is all too common. Once the cup is removed from the sanctuary of the machine, it quickly loses all structural integrity. This is much like a milk carton whose top has been completely opened and then recklessly filled to the brim with boiling oil. Try sticking your own mug in the dispensing bay of one of these guys and it will receive a small squirt of something foul while spraying you with scalding-hot water as the whole machine shuts down to await the attentions of its 'local' service engineer.

The engineer, of course, has three similar incidents to attend to this morning in his 120-mile call-out area.

Should you find yourself present when the engineer does finally turn up, whatever you do, don't look inside the machine. To do so is to gaze upon a forbidden nightmare world of pipes and fluid, far beyond our everyday comprehension. It's much like being the hapless witness to an alien autopsy. These people usually turn up with a couple of buckets and wearing waterproof footwear for a reason. It puts one more in mind of farmyard animals giving birth than a nice cuppa.

There is, of course, a certain starship captain who always gets his tea from his own personal vending machine built into his office wall. I suppose he thinks it's glamorous to have his own vending machine. As he only seems to drink Earl Grey then he is pretty safe as it all tastes like dilute aftershave, even if it has been molecularly assembled just for him.

 Christmas

Christmas is that special time of year between 6th November and 31st January during which, while remembering the birth of Christ, we are encouraged to spend as much money as we can afford. And then some more. Of course, if you just bought or received this book then that's perfectly fine.

It is also the time of year when whole communities come together with a shared purpose and vision for the festive season, which is to make their street visible from outer space. Any visiting aliens who were hoping to impress us with their UFOs bedecked with twinkling lights didn't reckon on Britain in December. I expect they all just park up on the moon over Christmas and do all those little jobs they've been putting off all year.

Tea, biscuits and cakes all play their part in the festivities. Back in the 1930s, tins of biscuits were all the rage as Christmas gifts. Nowadays, we still give tins of biscuits at Christmas, but rarely as your top, leave it until last, phone your mates up and boast about it sort of present. One of the most popular biscuit tins is the Danish Butter assortment. This, to me, is an enigma. What exactly is assorted about them? The Danes only appear to know how to make one type of biscuit, and in a feeble attempt to disguise this fact they make it in various shapes. Alas, most of the shapes are roughly circular, so any difference is far from obvious.

But the more troubling matter surely has to be Denmark's track record in biscuit baking. Granted, they are well known for their pastries, although it seems that everybody else makes them on their behalf, much in the way that the Spanish have franchised out their omelette business. There is also a lot of bacon of Danish origin. Biscuits, however are something that they only seem to crank out at Christmas. Presumably the Danish fleet of biscuit factories remains mothballed for much of the year and gets recommissioned each winter to produce a tide of butter biscuits. It also seems likely that the Danes put in a sizable order for butter round about mid-September, which could be a handy piece of information if you happen to run a dairy.

Many other well-known biscuit ensembles don a tin at Christmas, in much the same way that we put on our best jumper or frock. They are still the same old lovable biscuits, plus you have the bonus of a new biscuit tin. I always think it's nice to take the uneaten selections into the office at the end of January, just as the weather turns really nasty. By now, many people are subsisting on gruel and stale bread, having remortgaged their homes to pay for all the consumer electronics they bought at Christmas. During such times of hardship, a small foil-wrapped biscuit with a steaming cuppa can seem like the very lap of luxury. Perhaps it will help them look on the bright side: if their home does get repossessed, they can always live inside their new TV, most of which are now the size of small caravans.

Christmas simply wouldn't be Christmas without mince pies. These have seen a great deal of innovation over the years. The main advance has been the replacement of dangerous and unpredictable homemade ones with professionally made shop-bought ones. Christmas used to be a time when a bizarre arms race took place between Nanny Nicey and my aunties to create ever more durable and impervious mince pies. This would ensure that a small production run of mince pies would take weeks to work through, unless my dad was allowed unsupervised access to them. Nanny Nicey always insists that pastry tolerance is the cornerstone of any successful marriage. I suppose the same could be said of Wifey, given that she's never made pastry. She once made soda bread, which came out quite firm. I was tempted to phone up NASA and see if they could put the recipe to good use. Wifey said it was because she couldn't get hold of proper buttermilk.

Still, as a child I could sleep soundly at night, knowing that if the much-anticipated nuclear war broke out, we could improvise an effective fall-out shelter using upturned mince pies. Occasionally we would visit somebody who made mince pies with an even thicker and heavier-set pastry. After such visits, we were all supposed to feel thankful that the ones we were used to at least were rendered semi-pliable by scalding-hot tea.

 # Is it the End?

As a notorious biscuit enthusiast I'm often asked by people what happened to certain biscuits: 'Can you still get . . .?', 'Do they still make . . .?' and so on. I don't mind that at all, especially if I know the answer. Often a question such as 'Where can I get Lemon Puffs, I've not tasted them for thirty years?' can be answered by directing them to their local supermarket. They simply forgot to buy them for the last thirty years.

But there are others who are not so lucky, asking after McVitie's Royal Scot, Huntley and Palmer's Milk and Honey or Breakfast biscuits, Butter Osbornes, Banjo Wafers, Barmouth biscuits, Yoyos, Chocolate Garibaldis and even Abbey Crunch. Where are all these wonderful biscuits? Well, they are simply recipes and memories now. But what happened to them?

The chap eating his Lemon Puffs after a thirty-year hiatus doesn't worry that his long absence might have contributed to their downfall. For some biscuits, recipes were tinkered with and products lost their appeal. Others became uneconomic due to old production plants wearing out or the increasing cost of certain ingredients. With some brands, company mergers caused factories to shut and product ranges were rationalised. These are all factors that apply to virtually everything we consume; simple matters of supply and demand.

We have created a subtle and insidious rod for our own backs in the name of progress. Our love of the motor car is responsible for many of the changes we have seen in retailing and the products we buy. Large out-of-town shops are easily reached; we park there for free and fill our cars with bag after bag of shopping. By contrast, many years ago, I remember going shopping with Nanny Nicey, being dragged up and down the high street, waiting our turn at the butcher's, greengrocer's and the bakery.

Choice became a matter of how many shops you were prepared to visit, how far you wanted to walk and how much you could carry. No wonder I was quite old before I tasted a melon. So, yes, supermarkets with car parks were a boon, and people quickly took to the idea.

Now, though, we are reaping what we have sown. Town centres, for centuries the market-place for the local produce of a community, have been drained of their vitality. Bakers struggle to sell bread, cakes and pastries, having only a small passing trade of people who have come to visit their building society or to buy a birthday card. The outskirts of our towns have changed, too. Sprawling new estates, their detached houses packed closer together than terraced houses ever were, have no need of corner shops. They have been designed for the car, which demands ever more parking space. Gardens, an expensive waste of parking space, have dwindled to small postage-stamp-sized plots just big enough to accommodate a rusting barbecue. Estates are conveniently built next to a brand-new supermarket, which in theory can be reached on foot by eccentric pedestrians.

Vast stores create an illusion of choice so convincing that, if we can't find what we are looking for, we assume it's no longer made. As a result, we are eroding the diversity of our shopping experience. The retailers, of course, are only responding to our needs, and we can't really be too harsh on ourselves for wanting an easier life. As we rely on fewer and fewer chains, the range of products available to us becomes ever more refined and deliberated over by an ever-decreasing number of people.

Are we condemned to a gradual atrophying of real choice? Well, no, not at all, if that's not what we want. Already we are seeing consumers choosing to buy organic and Fair Trade products, and stores catering to this. Manufacturers who acquire smaller firms can often offer them the benefits of a larger European or even global distribution network for their products. Newly acquired products from around the globe can find themselves on our shelves alongside their established stablemates.

What can we do to help? Exercise our choice by trying new things, and look after the old favourites that you've not had in a while by buying some every now and again. Leave the car at home, and try walking to the corner shop for a few odds and ends. It may be frequented by elderly ladies, but they have a pretty good eye for a biscuit, and they'll make sure the shop-keeper gets all the good ones in. When you are next in town visiting the bank or buying a birthday card, pop into the bakery and get yourself some nice sticky buns, or some lemon curd tarts. You never know, you might even be able to get a nice cup of tea and a sit down while you are there. Lovely.

Acknowledgements

Our grateful thanks to all those who have helped with this book. First our agent Antony Topping for insisting that we do a book, and for all his help once he talked us into it. A special thanks to Denise Wilton for her lovely cup of tea, armchair and biscuit tin logos. To all those manufacturers who lent their support including United Biscuits, Fox's Biscuits, Burton's Foods, Bahlsen, Thomas Tunnock Ltd. To Barkers Bakery Ltd, Activehotels.com, Belly Busters Cafe for their assistance for the photography.

To all those who helped with the long and bizarre journey from office biscuit tin to book. Tony Wardell, Andrew Douglas, Eddie Hobson, Adam Reynolds, Rob Manuel, Joel Veitch, Nick Parker, Stephen and Mandy Borrill, Richard & Judy, Good Food Live, B4TA. To all the team at Time Warner Book Group, for their warmth and enthusiasm, and especially Tom Bromley for making the tea amongst other things.

Finally, of course, to all the biscuit-hunters, contributors and readers of NiceCupOfTeaAndASitDown.com whose input makes us both happy and proud at the very least twice a week, and remind us that we are actually very normal, especially Brian Barratt, Biscuit Man, James Fussell, Keith O'Kane and Maddalena Feliciello.